'My Sixteen Sisters'

Dancing with the Stars:
My Life as a Tiller Girl

by

Fay Robinson

This book is a work of non-fiction based on the life, experiences and recollections of Fay Robinson. In some limited cases, names of people, dates, places or details of events have been changed solely to protect the privacy of others. The author has stated that, except in such minor respects which do not affect the substantial accuracy of the work, the contents of this book are true.

All the photographs were kindly supplied by the author from her private collection.

Every effort has been made to obtain the necessary permissions with reference to acknowledging copyright material.

First Published 2014 by Appin Press, an imprint of Countyvise Ltd
14 Appin Road, Birkenhead, CH41 9HH

Copyright © 2014 Fay Robinson

The right of Fay Robinson to be identified as the author of this work has been asserted by her in accordance with the Copyright, Design and Patents Act 1988.

British Library Cataloguing in Publication Data.
A catalogue record for this book is available from the British Library.

ISBN 978 0 9926070 7 4

All rights reserved. No part of this publication may be reproduced, stored in a retrieval system, or transmitted, in any other form, or by any other means, electronic, chemical, mechanic, photograph copying, recording or otherwise, without the prior permission of the publisher.

Printed and bound in the UK by Birkenhead Press Ltd.
14 Appin Road, Birkenhead, CH41 9HH
www.birkenheadpress.co.uk

Overture

As I am now.

This is a memoir for an audience beyond my family and friends. I've had an extraordinary life, all achieved through hard work and determination.

I hope I have lived a life that some people only dream of.

Hard work I've never dodged away from, and I would always be looking for my next challenge or project. Sometimes life isn't fair, and there have been times when I've been incredibly unhappy. I then think there are people less fortunate than me, and I've hidden my unhappiness behind a sunny smile and thought of the things I have.

Whatever my failings, they have allowed me to rise from the dire poverty of post-war Yorkshire to a reasonably comfortable lifestyle, and even though my early childhood may have been a struggle, it was happy and loving most of the time.

I am not a star but my line of dancers were. I will unravel all the myths of this extraordinary line of famous dancers and how we all became sisters to each other.

Dedication

I must pay a special tribute to my family: my sister Jane, brothers Timothy and Jeremy, and sister-in-law Beverley, for their love and support, and to my dear mum and dad and grandparents who made all this possible and to whom I have dedicated this book.

This is how mum and dad remember me.

Acknowledgements

I am eternally grateful to all my friends and colleagues in the profession who have made my career such a happy and fulfilling one, many of whom are named in these pages, and to the many others who are not I proffer my apologies as well as my thanks. Sadly, some of them are no longer with us and I miss them all.

For their permission to mention them, my particular thanks to all my Tiller "sisters": Kath Darragh, Rosalie Kirkman, Hazel Stewart Brown, June Vincent, Silvia Blake Pamela Violet Keyes and Miss Wendy.

I'm sure everyone knows that if you are ever asked to give a speech and wanted to thank a few people, you will understand that you always end up leaving someone out.

David Wiseman and Jean Clarke I would like to thank you for many happy years working at the Night Out in Birmingham. Sandra and Roy Jones, Bruce Vincent and Wendy Clarke I can't thank enough for bringing the 60s Tiller Girls back together, and Dougie Squires for making it possible.

I'd like to thank Bruce Forsyth for inviting us to celebrate his seventieth birthday with him on a special Sunday Night at the London Palladium which had the wonderful Diana Ross as top of the bill. It was so nice to step out on that stage once again with such happy memories at a theatre where we always felt at home. Comedy was provided by the late Frank Carson and Ronnie Corbett. The bill was fantastic, and the show went out live that Sunday, just like old times.

Thanks to Dougie Chapman for giving me the opportunity to fulfil my dream and the late Robert Luff for giving us all permission to use the John Tiller Girls' name.

And thank you Peter Diamond and Jean Williams. Peter Diamond inspired me to write my autobiography. Whenever we met, he would say "have you written that book yet". He eventually persuaded me. A special tribute to Jean Williams without whose wonderful help and offer to type my story I couldn't have completed this personal project. She has been very supportive of me all the way, and I thank her for checking many of the details against my occasionally patchy memory.

I would like to thank Richard Birchall for many happy years working at the health club, and for respecting and trusting me and allowing me to go back to the Club to take a fitness class.

I have enjoyed a wonderful life making friendships I cherish deeply, many of whom appear in these pages. Those friendships are the most important reasons why I am happy to put all this on record.

Thank you to Peter Grant for his time, help and advice.

Finally, thank you my 16 sisters – and every audience who supported us.

SCENES		PAGE
ONE	The Year I Was Born	11
TWO	Grandparents	13
THREE	Family	17
FOUR	Childhood Years, What It Was Like	26
FIVE	On My Way	47
SIX	Tiller Girl Years at the Palladium	52
SEVEN	Working with the Stars	75
EIGHT	The History of our Mentor John Tiller and Our Schools	101
NINE	Tragedy, Tears and Laughter	112
TEN	By Royal Command	120
ELEVEN	Changing Direction	124
TWELVE	1960s Tiller Girls Reformed – Performing for Royalty	144
THIRTEEN	Moving on a Different Route	173
FOURTEEN	1960s Palladium Tillers My Trip to New York	180

FIFTEEN	Winning Line	186
SIXTEEN	Buckingham Palace Garden Party	197
SEVENTEEN	My Thousand Sisters	199
EIGHTEEN	A Love for My Work	209

Scene One

The Year I Was Born

The year I was born 1941 Britain's newspapers published the headline "Following attack on Pearl Harbour, US declares war on Japan and Sir Winston Churchill promises US immediate support".

The films showing that year were "The Road to Zanzibar" starring Bing Crosby and Bob Hope. Who would have thought that I would be working 17 years later at the London Palladium with Bob Hope topping the bill!

The Disney movie "Dumbo" opened in New York.

The German Jews were forced to wear the Star of David for easy identification, and National Service was extended to single women under 30 years old.

The top radio shows were *"Music While You Work"*, *"In Town Tonight"*, *"Workers Playtime"* and *"Radio Newsreel"*.

The songs of that year were The Glen Miller Sound with Chattanooga Choo Choo and A String of Pearls, Apple Blossom Time and Boogie Woogie Bugle Boy were sung by The Andrews Sisters.

The famous people born the same year as me were Paddy Ashdown, Bobby Moore, Jackie Collins and Mike Yarwood, the impressionist, who also shares the same birthday.

Half a dozen eggs cost nine pence (9d) equivalent to 4p today. Road tax for a car was seven pounds ten shillings (£7 10s 0d) equivalent to £7.50 today – how bizarre is that as some cars today are road tax free!

The average wage for a man was five pounds eleven shillings (£5 11s 0d) £5.57 per week, and for a woman it was two pounds fourteen shillings (£2 14s 0d) £2.70 per week.

I was born on 14 June 1941 one of seven children: four girls and three boys. I was next to the oldest. There was my older sister Anne Collette, myself, my brother Charles Michael who was severely mentally handicapped and suffered from epileptic fits, sister Lesley Rosemary, brother Timothy William, sister Antoinette Jane and brother Jeremy Thomas. Gosh! That was a lot to remember; I'm surprised I remembered all their names.

I had a different father to the rest of my brothers and sisters. My oldest sister was brought up by my gran and granddad, my mum's mum and dad. They had a three-bedroomed pit house in the small mining village of Harworth, South Yorkshire. My granddad was a miner having moved from a colliery in Barnsley. I grew up in this mining village of Harworth situated ten miles south of Doncaster.

I used to think my sister, Anne, was lucky as gran made her clothes and knitted her bonnets and jumpers. They took her on holidays to London and Jersey. I always thought she was fortunate, but I do remember granddad was so strict.

Scene Two

Grandparents

My gran and grandad.

My granddad was quite tall and distinguished looking, he had fair skin and silver white hair, just how you would expect a granddad to look. Some of his workmates used to call him "Snowball". He looked as if he might have been a high court judge or bishop. He was smartly dressed, and when wearing his suit with a matching waistcoat, he always had his 9 carat gold watch and chain in his waistcoat pocket. He had the watch chain made into two charm bracelets, one for mum and one for Aunt Brenda.

His hobbies were a flutter on the horses, a good debate on politics, of which he idolised Sir Winston Churchill, and reading books on William Shakespeare. He could make me laugh or cry with his sense of humour, and he could raise his voice and make you feel tearful.

Visiting my grandparents as a child holds a number of memories both happy and sad.

They had a piano which we were not allowed to touch. As a small child it was very tempting to tinkle with the keys. Neither gran nor granddad played the piano, but mum told me that when she was a little girl, she was learning to play it until gran became ill with meningitis and could not stand the noise, so she had to give up her lessons.

Granddad was a miner. This job he did after a short spell in London serving as a Coldstream Guard, and it became obvious to me why he liked his visits to London.

My mum and granddad had the same personalities and would often clash. When they had crossed words it was usually over money, but they soon made it up.

If mum had given me a note to give to gran to borrow money, gran would say "tell your mum I want it back and don't say anything to granddad". I used to think when I get to work, I'm never going to ask anybody for anything. I'll do it myself or do without. This is what I taught myself to do, especially when I feared the sound of granddad's voice when he was angry. I knew my gran understood; it was never any fault of mine. Granddad was extremely strict and seldom affectionate. Praise and encouragement were equally rare. It's fair to say that I was very frightened of him, and I'm sure he viewed us as a bit of a nuisance at times. He had very little patience. My gran must have had some hard times with him, but she never, ever, showed it.

My gran used to spoil me. Sometimes she would give me treats or a huge chunk of cake that she had baked herself. I learnt a lot from my gran; I thought she was a genius at making things. She always showed her love for me and never raised her voice. I loved her and thought the world of her.

I think if it hadn't been for my grandparents, mum and dad would have found it hard to support me with my dancing. I have a lot to thank my family for. Both mum and dad who struggled to bring up all my brothers and sisters and one being severely handicapped, and of course my grandparents, whom unaware to me at the time, must have helped tremendously.

One day when visiting my grandparents, my granddad came home from work looking like a black man. He put fear into me as he spoke in a funny voice. I had never seen a black man before, and I admit I was frightened. As a little girl I did not realise it was granddad covered in pit dust. He would make me laugh then go upstairs for his bath. I would then enjoy some quality time with my gran. I had never seen my dad covered in pit dust as he always showered at the pit before coming home from work. We never had the luxury of a bath so dad never had that choice.

My gran was a slim lady. She was very set in her ways. Wash day was always on a Monday, and there was bubble and squeak for a quick lunch from the leftovers from Sunday's dinner. Washing could take a whole day; there were no automatics or twin-tubs, it was the old washboards and hand wringers. There was a machine called a "mangle" with rollers for squeezing water from washed clothes. I remember as a very small child mum saying I nearly lost a finger on my right hand poking it at the cogs of the gear wheel of a mangle. My finger end had to be stitched back on. Gran's washing was spotless and her home was very clean. She had very good sewing skills and kept herself very smart. I can see her now on her "Singer" treadle sewing machine, which mum inherited and which came in handy for making my dancing costumes. It was gran and granddad who made me appreciate and look after things.

Gran made coats and bonnets for other children. She kept a notebook, and would go round to their homes and collect a few pence each week until their clothes were paid for.

Both gran and granddad enjoyed listening to the radio; there was no TV in those days. I had never heard of anyone in the village having a television. On some of my visits they would be listening to the *"Archers"*, *"Mrs Dale's Diary"* or sometimes it was Wilfred and Mabel Pickles in a programme called *"Have a Go"*. I remember if I was talking to gran, granddad would shout "be quiet!" He would make you feel uncomfortable as his voice was always very firm. They had a long wooden settee painted black. Gran had made bright coloured cushions for it, and granddad used to stretch out on it for a snooze after his dinner. It used to remind me of a church pew. I can see the blackout curtains hanging up at the windows, too, although I cannot remember much towards the end of the war apart from ration books and people not having much money. We could never afford holidays as a family, as other families did.

Gran and granddad had three daughters: my mum was the first born, then there was Aunt Phyllis and then Aunt Brenda. Aunt Brenda married a saddle maker; he made saddles for racehorses and animals for touring circuses. He made me a soft leather shoe bag for my ballet and tap shoes and a soft leather passport holder for my grandparents which I have inherited.

Aunt Phyllis met and married a French Canadian and they emigrated to Toronto Canada just after the war.

My gran's name was Bertha and my grandad's William Rose. I liked the surname Rose; it went well with another name. Ellen Lawson Rose was my mum's name before she married my father and Bertha Rose sounded nice too. My eldest sister even took the surname Rose when she was at school, probably because my grandparents brought her up.

Scene Three

Family

My mother, Ellen Lawson Rose, married my father, Wallace Robinson, at the Register Office in the district of Worksop in the county of Nottinghamshire in 1940; they were both twenty years old. My blood father I knew nothing about. He was, according to my birth certificate, a gunner in the Royal Artillery and then a butcher. I was born at my gran and granddad's house in Bircotes. He left mum and me when I was about two years old. I only found this out when mum passed away. She had left a letter from him in one of her old handbags. When I was looking through her belongings, I do believe she wanted me to see this letter. All my life she never spoke to me about him, or maybe she was too upset to tell me. I would have given her my support and love. This letter was a begging letter to ask mum for a divorce. In those days it wasn't so easy. I wondered why she never destroyed the letter. I felt it was something she wanted me to know about but never had the courage to tell me herself. I never ever saw my father, not even a photograph of him to see what or who he looked like.

In this letter my father said he didn't love mum, and had only stayed with her because of me. He said she didn't love him either so she should let him go. He even tried to make it easy by saying he had committed adultery, and gave the name and address of where it took place, and the lady's name. I think this hurt mum a lot, and I believe in my heart she was so hurt she wouldn't let him free and give him what he wanted (a divorce). He said if she couldn't manage me, he would take me. I'm glad she didn't let me go. I have no memories of my blood father apart from the letter I found in mum's old handbag and a card from him for my first birthday. This was the only birthday card mum kept. I wonder why.

When Mum was young she trained to be a nurse at St Luke's Hospital, Bradford. This was before she had me. I have a lovely photograph of her in her nurse uniform. When I was small, mum appeared to have a mountain of nursing books with sketches and drawings for her studying and homework. I regularly looked at the medical photos in her books. I couldn't read but I paid a lot of attention to how the human body functioned; so much so, that I cut out some of the photos from her books and stuck them on my bedroom wall, and, yes, I did get into serious trouble for it. Mum had books from her exams which her teacher had marked. Her drawings were so good. As I got older, I found her work fascinating and showed tremendous interest in her medical studies. I was very proud of her marks and teacher's comments. She was very attractive and beautiful.

My mum. St Luke's Hospital, Bradford, Looking smart in her uniform and remarkably like Margaret Thatcher, Prime Minister.

Mum was a very confident lady and didn't seem to fear anyone. She would speak her mind even though at times it would get her into trouble (especially with granddad or my dancing teachers). I certainly didn't take after her in that way. I never had the confidence she had, I wish I had. I was too shy and would bottle things up inside rather than say anything.

Mum was tall and slim, and like granddad had fair skin and blonde hair. Sometimes she reminded me of Margaret Thatcher, Prime Minister, and even looked like her on some photographs. She met a young man, Clarence Fullwood, and had five more children, my half brothers and sisters, but I only knew them as my brothers and sisters.

Me as a baby.

Sitting on the Air Raid shelter enjoying an apple with dad on the very top.

Me at school.

One day she went to my school to give my school teacher "a piece of her mind" for throwing a bunch of keys at me. I wasn't going to say anything to mum because I knew I wasn't paying attention in class. She noticed a mark on my face which was very close to my eye. Mum said "what's this on your face?" as she tilted my head back while brushing my hair. I said "it's nothing mum"; she said in a firm voice "nothing, what do you mean by that; where did you get that from?" I burst into tears because I hated her to think I'd been naughty. I said I'd leaned over to pick my pen up from the floor which had rolled off my school desk. As I came up I lifted my desk lid to put my pen away, and as I put the desk lid down, Mr Hildrith threw the keys which caught my face. This teacher was pretty well known for throwing things. It was whatever was handy; it could be a piece of chalk, the large blackboard rubber or, in my case, a bunch of keys. Mum was furious. I thought she was annoyed at me for misbehaving as she always used to say, if we were misbehaving in any way we deserved to be punished, but not by throwing a bunch of keys. She took me by the hand and marched me to school, and Mr Hildrith apologised. My brother came home from school after being disciplined and mum sent him back to add to his punishment for whatever reason; she said he deserved it.

Mum was always very particular about us all being well-mannered and polite. I guess after having seven children we had to be. We knew how far we could go before we got a clip round the ears, and we never answered back, well, only once, otherwise a sharp hand would flick across your mouth.

Clarence Fullwood, my stepfather, known only to me as a brilliant dad, was my father in every way, and I will refer to him as my dad. He was of average height for a man, very slender and had little hair. He was bald on top and thinning round the sides. We could all make fun of him and he would take it in good spirit. Dad was so laid back and easy going; he loved children and would never argue or upset anyone. He was very young when he lost his mother, and his father re-married a lady a lot younger than him whom we used to call auntie.

As a child I only had one set of grandparents on my mother's side of the family. Dad had two brothers, Uncle Charlie and Uncle Doug. Uncle Charlie lost one of his legs in the war. His false leg had little holes in it, and, as children do, we used to roll his trouser bottom up and poke matches into them. We were all very fond of Uncle Charlie.

At Christmas mum would ask one of us to go round to Uncle Charlie's and ask for one of his stump stockings to hang on the bottom of our bed for Father Christmas to fill with an apple, orange, sweets and nuts. As we got older, the stump stocking wasn't big enough, and as the family was increasing, there weren't enough stockings to go round, so it developed into a pillowcase.

One Christmas my brother, Timothy, got "Muffin the Mule" which he was very happy playing with. My other brother, Jeremy, was very young and more interested in the huge cardboard box it came in.

When I was ten years old I still believed in Father Christmas. I was getting a bike and said to mum "how's he going to get it down the chimney?" Then my older sister spoilt it and said "don't be silly, it's your mum and dad that do it while you are asleep".

In my eyes, my stepfather, my mum's partner, was always my father. He loved mum and he was my DAD. A wonderful man, hardworking, and would do anything for us. Mum used to call him 'Tiny' and so did all his family, his real name was Clarence. Mum's name was Ellen, Dad used to call her Nellie. It seems in those days everyone had a nickname. My sister Lesley was 'Spider' and my youngest sister Toni Jane was called 'Flue Brush'; this was because when she was born she had a mop of hair that stood up like a brush.

Dad would do the washing, ironing, cooking, cleaning and make the most fantastic Yorkshire puddings. Later on in life, on Sundays he would cook our breakfast. In fact, I wouldn't get out of bed until I smelt the bacon crisping. He was a coal miner, too, like his dad and my granddad. They all worked shifts down the mines as it paid extra money. Our cooked breakfast on a Sunday was quite a treat, and I used to look forward to it.

Like gran, mum was also good at cooking and sewing. She used to say, 'I can't save money baking bread for you lot'. As soon as she took it from the stove we would eat it hot with the butter melting. I, too, must have picked up a few skills sewing and knitting because I have made quite a few of my own clothes, knitted coats and dresses.

First Home "A Hut"

We must have moved from gran's when I was about three years old. We went to live in my dad's stepmother's front room. I think this is where Michael, my brother, was born. When I was five years old we got our own home: an RAF hut down a narrow track into Swinner Wood. We had no hot water, no electricity or flushing toilet. The loo was a smelly shed with a resulting appalling pong. For our bathroom, we had the usual tin bath. Water was heated on the stove for our weekly bath. As a child you don't understand how poor you are, but when you get older you'll do whatever it takes to avoid feeling humiliation.

A blind man lived on the site, we called him Blind Billy, and he used to frighten us by tapping his stick along the side of our hut at night. I was very frightened at night in the dark; there weren't any lights in the woods. It was very spooky. You could hear weird bizarre noises which became familiar during the dark nights.

The walk to school seemed never-ending; it took us about forty minutes. It was so very, very cold and mum used to wrap me up with a big scarf, cross it over my chest, and tie it behind my back. We also wore our liberty bodices over our vests (which had rubber buttons down the front). I used to call them my corsets.

When I was six years old I became very ill. I had a fever of 102°F and the glands in my neck were enlarged. I had a sore throat and began to vomit, sweat and shiver. I was rushed to an isolation hospital where it was discovered I had scarlet fever which was caused by a streptococcus germ. A century ago it was regarded as one of the major killers of children, but nowadays it seems to have changed its nature. Thank goodness. I remember having to drink this awful liquorice powder out of a white tin mug; the smell and taste made me sick. I got so used to the smell of Dettol. Visiting times were strict, with mum and dad visiting on their own again as children weren't allowed.

When I was seven we moved from the hut in the woods to another RAF hut, this time it was just off the main road and more like a camp with air raid shelters. It was nearer to the village of Harworth so it made my walk to school shorter.

When I was small I was very shy and wasn't very confident. Mum took me to a local dancing school at Tickhill; it was a short bus ride away from Harworth. Most nights after school I would help Mum, and I would always end up running for the bus. It was my job to get the tea ready, usually a potted meat or jam sandwich and a slice of jam roll.

My dancing school was very Victorian; our teachers were very strict and we were frightened of them. They were perfectionists and we wouldn't dare ask for a night off. My teachers were twins, Miss Maud and Miss Eunice Ashmore. Their mother, Mrs A, used to help out in class. We weren't allowed to do anything other than dance; swimming or being invited to birthday parties were out of the question.

One of the pupils, a boy about eight years old, was rehearsing for a competition and he forgot his lyrics for his song. He said "I forgot it Miss". Mrs A got hold of him at the back of his collar and dragged him up the room - his feet never touched the floor. Their attitude was: if you want to dance, you will dance! Mrs A was petite, and although a tiny lady, she was strong.

Me with my dancing teachers and Mrs A in Blackpool, 1957.

On another occasion I was doing the splits, and we were supposed to be practising ballet. My teacher walked into the room and instructed me to stay there: "if that's what you want to do", and made me stay in the splits for a good 15 minutes.

My teachers wouldn't allow you to attend their school to play around. If they saw potential in a pupil they would work hard to bring the best out in them. They were even known to help financially with any child so as not to hold them back. They were very proud teachers.

Scene Four

Childhood Years - What It Was Like

I wanted to dance, and like all little girls my dream was to be a ballerina. When I started my dancing lessons, my teachers pointed out to mum that I appeared to have a problem with my back. I had to work extra hard to overcome what felt to me like a handicap of not being able to bend equally or evenly backwards without twisting to one side. I wasn't a natural at being flexible like most small children; I couldn't even sit crossed legged on the floor because of the stiffness in my spine. I've never been able to do this or achieve it from hard work. My teachers said I would be in serious trouble when I got older if I didn't try and bend equally. They were so right.

I went through lots of stretching, bending and pulling by my dancing teachers. I used to lie on my tummy on the floor, and my teachers would take my hands over my head and pull me backwards to try and reach my ankles. The pain was pretty horrific at times; it was so bad, I fought to hold back the tears. My teachers hated you to cry and would say they were crocodile tears. They had been known to send you home if you didn't take the discipline. I felt sore and stiff sometimes, but their answer would be "well, do it again, that will get rid of the pain". Mum was told to rub linseed oil into my joints to loosen them. It made you feel better, but I think that was from the massage. Dancing seemed a way of escape from what I thought was my duty of helping mum look after my handicapped brother Michael.

*Tap pose.
Taken outside our hut.*

*Ballet pose.
Taken outside our hut.*

*Smart Soldier.
Taken outside our hut.*

I was frightened and terrified mum would stop me dancing because she knew how much pain I was going through; so much so that I never told her what I had been put through in class. I never told her how I felt I was struggling with the fight and battle I had to gain the movement required.

To dance, that was all I wanted to do, and all I thought I could do. It was sheer hard work and determination, and being educated didn't interest me at all. I didn't mind missing school and looking after Michael because I knew mum would be able to work extra hours and it would help to pay for my dancing lessons. I sometimes worried how they would find the money for me.

As a child, I was always trying to fix things to make situations better. Today I would have been classed as a child carer, and there would have been lots of help available. One day mum ran out of soap. She didn't have any money to send me to the shop, and asked me to go next door to hut number 9 to Aunt Rhoda's. She wasn't my aunt really, but we called all our neighbours "auntie" or "uncle". Mum said ask Aunt Rhoda if I can borrow a bar of soap until the week-end. Aunt Rhoda gave me a bar of Imperial Leather and the perfume from it was beautiful.

Aunt Rhoda and Uncle Les didn't have any children. She helped mum quite a lot and would spoil us, especially my sister, Lesley, and me. When I was about eight or nine years old, we went to the cinema to see the film "The Red Shoes". This was a treat from Aunt Rhoda for my birthday. Our village cinema was a huge shed type building which we would call "the pictures" or "the flix". The film inspired me even more, and I was obsessed by Moira Shearer, the ballet dancer. I think this was the first film I ever went to see, or maybe because of my love for dance, it was the only one I remember. At the end of the film, I walked home in tears because

Moira Shearer had thrown herself under the train. It was so sad. I don't remember seeing any more films when I was a child.

A Troupe Costume.

*Easter Parade costume.
Age 10.*

My acrobatic.

A little bit bendy.

In 1953 my dancing school was asked to appear at the Albert Hall, London. The school was one of many schools and the arena was full of children; I was one of them. I think I was eleven years old, and I remember mum being sent a letter asking her permission for me to be able to go. We were given a letter in class and told to make sure mum got it as it was urgent. Our parents were delighted, and even if they couldn't afford it, they would find the cash from somewhere. Travelling was usually a visit to my gran's when granddad would say "does your mother think we are made of money?"

Dress rehersal for the Albert Hall.
Age 12.
I'm the one without a costume.

This was my first trip to the Big City, London. We travelled down by coach; I know it felt a very long way. The journey was so long, it was like moving to a different country. On arrival at the Albert Hall, I couldn't believe my eyes - the building was huge. When we were rehearsing in the huge arena we would get lost entering and leaving as the steps to the arena went off in all directions. At times we couldn't find our dressing room, too. During dress rehearsal I was the only one without a costume; mum hadn't finished mine, so I wore my class outfit. Mum was in the dressing room sewing trying to get my costume finished.

During my dancing school years, I took lots of exams and entered dance competitions up and down the country. I took most of my exams and passed with very good marks - 90s and 95s out of a 100! But in nearly every report it said I needed to smile more. I know most of the time it was because I was shy. But I loved my dancing. I hardly ever played out. I didn't seem to have the time. I played in the air raid shelters, using one as a dressing room, coming up the steps out onto the grass and doing cartwheels and rollovers while my friends were watching. They would sit on the side of the shelter and so did my dad sometimes. I used to pretend I was on stage and they would applaud. By doing this, I could always tell my dancing teachers that I had practised.

One day when walking home from school with my friend, as we approached the gate to her home, which had a narrow footpath that led to her house, she waved and said "ta rah Fay, see you tomorrow". I remember thinking, my home is a black hut down a dirt track of a road with big holes in the muddy path which sometimes were filled with rainwater. I wondered what it would be like to live in a proper house. Sometimes it made me feel deprived and that our family wasn't good enough, then I would think it was because of my handicapped brother, Michael, and this made me sad. There didn't appear to be another family that had a brother like mine. I used to think this was special, and I knew things were different. We never took friends home to play. Michael used to entertain himself in the back garden making holes in the soil and filling his trouser pockets with creepy crawlies and things. He liked to waddle a stick up and down while he made a funny noise.

Michael spent most of his time digging and making sand pies in the garden which was surrounded by a wire netting fence so he wouldn't wander off. We were never able to have any pretty coloured flowers in our garden. One day this must have had some effect on me and I did a very naughty thing. I saw someone's front garden looking beautiful, and I found myself walking down their path and picking the flowers, tulips and daffodils, from their garden. I ran home hoping no-one had seen me, not realising the flowers wouldn't grow without the roots, and planted them in our garden. Yes, I got a hiding from mum and was sent to bed, and was threatened with "if it happens again, she would ban me from my dancing for a couple of days". I knew then I would be in trouble with my dancing teachers. She also said she would take me to the person's house and tell them it was me. Mum always kept to her word,

Picture of my special brother Michael, age 3, with dad.

My brother Michael with teddy, age 6.

and we only ever misbehaved once. I remember Jeremy biting my nephew on his arm so mum got Jeremy's arm and bit him back so he could feel what pain had been endured.

Michael looking a bit annoyed at getting his photo taken. Me and dad trying to keep him still. Dad's pit socks showing in the breeze.

I asked mum if I could have a cat. She said no because they took a lot of looking after and were too expensive. I said I would look after it and it wouldn't cost anything. Mum said "and who is going to feed it?" I said dad because I knew he would, but mum still said no. I then forgot all about it until one day on my usual walk home from school, which took about twenty minutes, I saw this cute black cat. It had a stump for a tail. It happened to cross my path: good luck at last perhaps? I called it and it came to me. I made a fuss of it; I loved it and picked it up; it was so beautiful and cuddly so I carried it home. When I arrived home, just before I opened the door, I placed it on the floor. As I walked in, it followed me, then mum said "where did you find that?" I said "nowhere mum, it just followed me home. It's going to be lucky for us because it's black."

Me with my furry friend Tibby.

Mum looked at dad with a smile on her face, and I was hoping they would let me keep it, and they did. Mum did say I should first go back to where I found it to see if I could find out who it belonged to, but I never did. I was really happy with my little furry friend that I named Tibby. Dad used to order a bag of "lights" from the butchers, which were the giblets of animals and only cost a few pence, for Tibby's food. Some days when walking home from school I would do cartwheels. My mum's friend said one day to mum "I always know when Fay's passing, I see two feet in the air". Cartwheeling or walking on my hands – that was me.

On the odd occasion we played out, we used to entertain ourselves playing games. A piece of chalk, small stones, tin cans, marbles and skipping ropes were our usual play things. With the chalk we would draw squares on the pavement. In the centre we would write a number, and all we would need was a flat stone to push or slide along the pavement into a square, then we would hop on one leg and pick up the stone. This game was called hopscotch, and I could only play it at my friend's house because we never had a road or flat surface where I lived. A game called "snobs" was played using small stones gathered from the garden. I think we had about six or seven. We would sit on the pavement, throw the stones into the air, catch them on the back of our hand, then throw them up again to see how many we could catch.

As a treat on Sundays we usually had a tin of fruit for tea. We would ask mum to save the empty tins but sometimes we rescued them from the dustbin. Dad would rinse them out and put two small holes in each side. We would tie rope or strong string through the holes and turn them upside down. Then we would stand on them (one for each foot), hold on to the rope and use them to walk on like stilts. It was good fun.

Marbles were all bright colours and different sizes. We used to roll them into small holes we had made in the garden, and swap them if someone had an unusual one for another marble or sweets.

My favourite was skipping as it was more energetic and where my dancing skills came in handy. Skipping was more of a girlie thing, and something the boys weren't that good at. We used to skip in the school playground. I was quite a star at French skipping when we used two skipping ropes together. I was also pretty good at jumping over the rope, and on sports days I'd developed quite a good skill and technique for the high jump. My schoolteacher encouraged me and saw potential, and I was chosen by our school to take part in the whole of the area of Nottinghamshire Sports Day representing our school. I won first place and became Nottinghamshire High Jump Champion. I didn't have a particular style only the scissor movement like a hitch kick over the bar.

If I was going to take sport a stage further and maybe make a career of it, I was going to have to train hard and develop a better style and technique. This I didn't want to do because of my love of dance. I'd made my mind up what I was going to do when I left school.

My oldest sister had a little black doll she cherished; she called her Black Sally. It was unusual to see a black doll and it was so cute and perfect. My grandparents had bought it for her. I had a doll quite a lot bigger than my sister's which my brother, Michael, got hold of and broke its arms and legs. I was very upset at the time, but of course it was my fault for leaving it where Michael could get hold of it. Aunt Rhoda took it along to the dolls' hospital in Doncaster to get it mended. This was a shop on Hall Gate where all little girls had their dollies made better.

It was a struggle at times for mum and dad. Dad worked shifts down the pit and mum had started a part-time job at the Crown Hotel, Bawtry, working mornings. I had to wash my underwear and socks as I didn't have many clothes; I used to rub them in a towel so they would dry overnight. Once my shoes had a hole in the sole, so I put a piece of cardboard inside. I didn't complain to mum or dad because I wanted any spare cash for my dancing.

Michael, who was autistic, needed a lot of attention; he couldn't be left on his own. There was no help in those days. I missed quite a bit of schooling helping Mum look after him. This was so Mum could go to work in the mornings, while I was waiting for dad to come home from night shift.

My school reports were often marred by poor attendance. Dad used to go to bed at lunchtime when mum came home from work. If he was home in time I would go to school in the mornings, but this only happened on the odd occasion, and only the week he was on nights. Mum and dad seemed to be always working. We never had any books so they never read stories to us. It seemed we couldn't have anything that Michael could destroy.

Copy of my school report.

NOTTINGHAMSHIRE EDUCATION COMMITTEE
BIRCOTES
THE NORTH BORDER SECONDARY SCHOOL.

REPORT

Name: Fay Robinson Date: March '55
Form: 3/3 Age: 13 yrs 9 mts

Subject	Max	Act'l	Remarks
English	60	15/20	
Arithmetic	50	Abs	
Geography	20	Abs	
History	20	Abs	
Science	-	-	
Scripture	20	Abs	
Music	20	Abs	
Art	A	B-	
Hygiene	-	-	
Physical Education	A	A	
Rural Science (Biology)	20	1-2	
Woodwork	-	-	
Metal Work	-	-	
Technical Drawing	-	-	
Housecraft	20	15	
Needlework	20	19	
	210	61/80	

No. in Form: 41   Conduct: Excellent.
Position: —   Attendance: F. Good
           Punctuality: Excellent

TEACHER'S REPORT Fay is a very neat and tidy girl. Further, she is capable of good work. Unfortunately, however she is held back through absence from school.

.................J. H. Higgins............... Class Teacher
.................CH Almay.................... Head Master

Living here in this 'hut', I recall when it rained we had to put saucepans and buckets in different rooms to catch the rain water coming in from the roof. I know one day we had no pans for cooking as they were in use - catching rain water. It was very cold as the floors were concrete and covered in lino. You could hear the dripping of the water.

We still had no electricity, but we did have paraffin lamps. Dad used to hang them up. Hot water was still heated on the stove for our weekly bath. Outside we had a block of toilets; there were about three which the whole camp would share. The toilet paper was newspaper cut into pieces which was kept on string on the back of the toilet door.

We kept hens and sometimes geese on this camp. I hated them as they used to chase me. We used to eat one for Christmas dinner. The rest were given to other families living on camp for Christmas. The geese used to wander round the camp site pecking on people's doors for bread. They would turn round, run up the dirt track and actually take flight. I was hoping they would fly off, but they always landed.

As most food was still on ration we had ration books. Happily sweets came off ration. We would go to the village sweet shop but the queue was very long. I enjoyed my three-penneth of dolly mixtures and a huge gobstopper that changed colours, and I loved the pineapple chunks, pear drops and aniseed balls. They were given to us in a small bag shaped like a cornet.

Mum was a good cook and we always had good food. She could bake a meal for us all out of a tin of corned beef or egg. She would make sure we always had fruit and veg. The fruit and veg came round by horse and cart, and mum used to go out with a bucket and buy lots. She would make her own fruit salad in a huge bowl and I would help her.

When I was twelve we were still living on camp. I was doing quite well by then with my dancing. Money was tight; I hated it sometimes when mum asked me to go to gran's to borrow money, and it was usually for me for exams, new ballet shoes or material for dancing costumes. I would never ask mum for anything, but it was always me that mum sent to gran's in case granddad and her had crossed words. I always knew gran would help if she could. I would have done without anything not to have to keep going to gran's.

Sometimes Mum would get a clothes cheque from the Co-op and pay it back weekly. I had all my dance classes on the tick! That's what we called it in those days. Monday ballet, Wednesday show or competition work, Thursday private lesson and Friday was tap and acrobatic. Mum paid for my lessons on Friday night when Dad had been paid. She sometimes gave me 3d extra for chips, as a treat.

While living here in our 'hut for a home', my sister Lesley was born. She was a beautiful baby and mum kept her in pretty clothes that she'd made; everyone came round to see her. Her sewing skills came in handy. Mum then found herself making things for other people which all helped with extra pennies.

Dad hired a TV for the Coronation. We had everyone on camp in to see it; of course it was a very small screen and in black and white. All the children sat on the floor with some cats on their laps. Some adults were seated with the remainder standing.

Our school holidays I used to look forward to, not because there was no school, but because Mum used to do work in the fields pea picking. When we were off school, mum found work so she could take us along with her. The only snag was that we had to be up early – 6 am. It was great fun having the tractor pick us up in the trailer, and we enjoyed our picnic in the fields. Mum got paid by how many bags of peas she could pull. Our treat in the holidays was a one day trip to Cleethorpes or a seaside place on the east coast. It was usually on a Sunday and organised by the pit where dad worked. On mum's pea picking days I always had to go along to look after Michael and keep an eye on the baby who was Lesley. My Mum made all my dancing costumes. Some that stand out in my mind include a red velvet dress with white swansdown round the hem and sleeves. I also had a white off-the-shoulder dress with coloured frills on for 'over the rainbow', and my acrobatic costume was a black all-in-one covered in coloured sequins. On some occasions I was worried as I was always the last to get my costume finished, but mine usually turned out to be the best in the end. I think mum used to like to surprise them. One night I fell asleep and Mum woke me to try my costume on. She would stay up all night to get my costumes finished and always put that special detail on them. She was ambitious for me and wanted me to stand out from the rest. My problem was I was painfully shy and would bottle things up. I would pretend I was happy even if I wasn't, especially when I couldn't play out with my friends because I was looking after Michael.

When I was about thirteen years old we moved into our first house, a brand new council house. It was amazing - hot water, electricity and a bathroom, what a luxury. Our first house was like a dream compared to where I'd grown up. My sister Jane and brothers Timothy and Jeremy were born here. My brother Michael, who was also epileptic, went to a private hospital in Newark so my parents could have a respite. He was getting too big and strong now the little ones had arrived, and our house wasn't big enough.

Dad had a gate put on the side of the house when Michael returned from hospital. He disappeared on a number of occasions when someone left the gate open, and we had to walk the streets looking for him. He was then accepted into the hospital permanently. Mum and dad went to visit him. They had to get a taxi every time as it was about 33 miles away and awful to get to if you didn't have a car. There was no direct public transport.

Michael became very poorly having frequent epileptic fits and falling quite badly. He then got pneumonia. Having received a telegram, mum and dad were called out in the middle of the night. Michael had passed away aged twenty-one years.

I was doing better at school, but I wished I'd worked harder. I was good at sport, having won the Nottinghamshire high jump championships. I won a writing competition at school and always got good marks for maths and sewing. On a number of occasions I came top in my exams. I left school at fifteen years old with no academic qualifications. Coming up to fifteen years old, Mum was asked to go to see my dancing teachers, along with a few other mothers, to discuss what they wanted their daughters to do. My Mother wanted me to be a 'TILLER GIRL' at the Palladium. Some other mothers picked the Royal Ballet School, but, in mum's eyes, dancing at the Palladium and being on television was the highest achievement a dancer could accomplish.

In 1956, at fifteen years old and a very young fifteen years old, I was still in white ankle socks which I came out of overnight and into my stockings and suspender belt. I went down to London for three auditions. It was suggested that I took three together, hoping I would get at least one. I went to the John Tiller School, Italia Conti School and the Joan Davis School, and I got offered all three in one afternoon. I charged across London in a taxi with my dancing teacher putting demands on me: "Do this, do that, and don't forget to smile". I had never ever stayed away from home before.

I accepted the Joan Davis contract because it was near home - a pantomime in Leeds. I suppose mum might have been disappointed as she wanted me to be a 'Tiller Girl' but she didn't show it. For this contract, I was offered £6 10s 0d (six pound ten shillings) per week, working 6 days, Monday to Saturday with Sundays off. It was a lot of money to me, as dad only got nine or ten pounds per week working down the mines. I did send a few shillings home to help Mum and Dad. Granddad had a chat with me before I started my panto. It has stuck in my mind ever since; he said, "Now then, when you get paid make sure you save ten shillings (10s 0d) a week". So I did, and I still do.

My pantomime had lots of star names in it and, of course, Fay Robinson! The press had the story, three auditions in one day, Fay fifteen years old and walked it! Also saying I was a school girl and a miner's daughter from Harworth. I felt proud for mum and dad. Dad said all the lads at work were talking to him about me. I felt like a little star in the village. Everyone rallied round: my parents, grandparents, aunts, uncles and my dancing teachers, all helping mum to get things together to send me off on my journey.

3 auditions in day (Press copy)

3 auditions in a day —Fay (15) "waltzed" it

Y.E. NEWS REPORTER

THREE London auditions in one afternoon . . . it was enough to give a veteran stage fright. But not 15-year-old schoolgirl, Fay Robinson, a miner's daughter, of Windermere Avenue, Harworth.

Not fair-haired, green-eyed Fay. Victrix Ludorum of Harworth Secondary School, house captain, Nottinghamshire County schools high jump champion and horse captain.

She raced from one audition to the other, from the West End to the East End of London, and she "waltzed" through all three.

She was offered three contracts between 12.30 p.m. and 5 p.m. It was like a dream come true.

TURNED THEM DOWN

She turned down contracts with famous impresario John Tiller, and Davies' Dramatic, Stage, Screen and TV School, London.

She signed a contract with Davies' Theatrical, Stage, Screen and Radio School, because they could arrange for her to appear in pantomime at Leeds this Christmas —" and I didn't want to go too far from home."

If she had accepted the other contracts she would have had to work in London.

" I was very excited, but not the least bit nervous," Fay said to-day, adding that she did not find her "marathon" of ballett, acrobatic, tap, modern musical, musical comedy and modern ballet dance routines "any strain at all."

Fay's teacher, Miss Eunice Ashmore of Tickhill, described her as " brilliant."

Her headmaster attributed Kay's success on both stage and sports field to " co-ordination, perfect co-ordination. Some people have, and some don't. Fay has it."

Before my rehearsals for my panto in Leeds, I spent a few weeks in London at the Joan Davis School. I stayed at the Theatre Girls Club in Greek Street, Soho. Joan Davis had her office almost next door. I had never left home before so I didn't go out at night in case I got lost. After dinner I would sit on the window sill and watch 'those ladies' walking up and down Greek Street. They had very short skirts and high heels or boots on, and lots of make-up. I had never heard of prostitution. I just wondered why they were doing it! I feared the big city, London; I thought I would get lost coming from a quiet small mining village and never going far. London was a huge city to conquer.

The Theatre Club had three or four floors, a washing house and chapel on the top floor. The rooms were very tiny, like a hospital ward. The lady that ran the Club was called Miss Bell; she had long silver grey hair which she wore up in a bun. At meal times she would ring the bell. One night some other dancers who were staying there were having a séance. I didn't take part but I was intrigued, so I watched. When one of them said, "Is there anybody there?" there was a quiet spell and then the light went out. In walked Miss Bell in her white nightdress, long hair brushed down from her bun and shouted, "What are you doing?". Of course the lights should have been out by 10.30 pm. It was really scary. I can recall that just outside the tiny chapel upstairs there was a picture of Jesus; it seemed to be printed on material. If you stared long enough at it without blinking, his eyes used to open and close. That was frightening. Some cubicles were only separated by a curtain, the space just big enough for a bed, and you had to wash and do your washing on the top floor.

My dancing teachers' mother used to send me parcels with goodies and cakes she had made for me. I looked forward to that. I couldn't wait to open them. Miss Maud and Miss Eunice were very proud of me; they knew I'd worked very hard to achieve my goals and their mother, Mrs Ashmore, always used to say they were there for me if ever I needed anything. I would phone them quite regularly. We didn't have a telephone and mum wasn't good at writing to me. Sometimes I used to think they wanted to take me over. I don't mean adopt, but I always felt they knew mum and dad couldn't give me what they could financially, and even offered to take me on holiday with them. It could have been their way of showing how proud of me they were.

I never wanted mum or dad to feel hurt in any way, and I found myself trying to juggle my love accordingly without upsetting anyone. When I went home some week-ends, I always found time to visit them. It was hard really because they would do or say anything to prevent me from leaving. I learnt to say I was going at least one or two hours before I'd planned to. They never wanted to let me go.

Scene Five

On My Way

My pantomime in Leeds was my very first professional engagement, it was also a time for me to experience living away from home.

My first day of rehearsals was at 10 am at the Leeds Grand Theatre on 10 December 1956. The pantomime was "Jack and the Beanstalk" and starred Brian Reece, Joan Regan and Audrey Jeans. Comedy was provided by Jimmy James, Roy Castle and Bretton Woods. They were three very funny stooges. Although they all had separate roles to play in the pantomime, they performed an act together. Jimmy James would have a cigarette hanging from his mouth, Roy Castle wore a long army type coat and carried a shoe box under his arm, while Bretton Woods hardly said anything, but he was very thin, tall and had a very long neck. I know the tag line in their act was always "IN THE BOX". Bretton Woods would say to Jimmy James that he had an elephant for a pet. Jimmy would say "Don't be silly, where would you keep an elephant" and they would say "IN THE BOX".

Roy Castle was a brilliant entertainer. He could sing, dance and play the trumpet, and he would practise whenever he had a moment to spare. He would have his tap shoes on and would be tapping outside the dressing rooms and along the corridor. He did this in between the matinee and evening performance. It was very tragic and a great loss to our profession when he passed away. As Tillers, we have done many charity shows for his appeal.

It was during my pantomime season that I had to join the actors union called Equity. You couldn't perform in London or on television unless you were an Equity member. There was an annual fee which some of us paid in instalments. An Equity representative called to collect it each week, and by the end of our season I had paid my year's subscription.

I'd also learnt during this season that the colour green was unlucky for show business people. I don't know why other than when we wore green ballet dresses for one of our routines, as I ran forward I slipped onto my backside and nearly ended up in the orchestra pit. One of the girls said it was because green was an unlucky colour and it was superstitious.

Boy dancers seemed to be in short supply. I know because I was always chosen to play the boy's part. I used to long to be a girl and wear pretty dresses and petticoats, and wear my lovely long hair in curls. But no, I was a boy in knickerbockers, hair up under a hat and with a white shirt with bishop sleeves and waistcoat. I know I was tall, but I was beginning to get a complex about my figure.

Me as a boy dancer. "Lovely bishop sleeves"

Obsessed With My Body

I was going through a bad patch in my teenage years. It was just before I re-auditioned for the Tiller Girls and I was nearly sixteen years old. It was like peeling an onion's skin layer after layer; it brought tears to my eyes thinking of my body shape and lack of confidence. I seemed to live in fear of not being good enough to achieve anything and it became a fight with myself. It played a huge part in my shyness.

I was now nearly sixteen years old, and like most teenagers I was obsessed with the way I looked. Some problems life has a nasty habit of throwing at us. Generally, these issues: a chronic lack of confidence or, say, a phobia, have spiralled out from something in our teenage years. I hated my body. I seemed to be a late developer, and must have been at the end of the queue when "boobs" were given out.

I was tenderly nursing several oversized grudges, but the most corrosive current one was the phobia over my small bust. How often have we looked back and regretted things we didn't achieve because of lack of confidence. I always found it easy to say no; however, I nursed the feeling I was a failure after embracing my fear that 'I would be alone for ever'.

My dancing teachers (being very Victorian in attitude) always gave us the impression that having a boyfriend was a dirty word, and that when you showed interest in boys, your dancing days were over. They made it clear they did not approve. Neither did the John Tiller Schools.

I always shied away from parties; not only did I not have the confidence to mix very well, I didn't drink, I hated the taste of wine, and I had this knotty, tangled complex over the way I looked. I wanted to always be in control of what I was doing, and yet I could perform on stage and dance my legs off to my heart's content. It was a number of years before I could accept the way I looked; in fact I was 22 years old. I felt people thought I was unsociable.

During my summer season in Brighton one of our Tiller Girls introduced me to an air steward who worked for British Airways. It sometimes takes more confidence than one can conjure up to say yes to a date, but I did. The fear of rejection is a potent little poison; the dread of being laughed at stifles us all. I feared I would be wearing a padded bra for the rest of my life. What I needed at work and in life was a confidence boost.

I felt tongue-tied by my sense of inferiority. Yet, I accepted my date which took a lot of courage. I didn't want to hold hands, and I didn't want to be kissed or touched. The dirty word 'boys' was at the back of my mind! After two or three dates and my season finished, for me, that was it. But he came to see me on my next contract. I felt he was going to make himself a nuisance. He wanted me to give up show business, just when I was enjoying the success of it. After all, dancing was my first love. So I finished with him. I didn't feel comfortable and it didn't feel right, and I had my eye on someone else.

As the years went by, I learnt to accept me as I was. After all, it wasn't holding me back career-wise. I was getting all the best work a dancer could get and I was signing contract after contract.

I began to realise that having small breasts was an advantage for a dancer. By now, I'd realised other dancers with large bosoms always had problems. One could always make a bust bigger but you couldn't make it smaller, and as lots of ladies, not just dancers, complimented me on my figure and tiny waist, I began to grow to like it and to love the skin I was in. Now I just felt I had a dancer's body, and made fun of my own small bust.

It was convenient working my pantomime so near to home, and I realised then why I didn't accept the Tillers in the first place. It was because Miss Barbara Aitken, the lady who auditioned me, lifted my hair up and said "this will have to come off". To work as a Tiller Girl you had to have short hair. It was written in our contracts. I understand now the way Miss Barbara chose her girls; they had to be used to discipline, strict rules and behaviour. Being used to discipline from my dancing school, I fitted the scene.

With Christmas 1956 over and my pantomime season finished, my mum's dream was about to come true, and my life ruled by discipline was about to continue.

Scene Six

"Tiller Girl Years" At The Palladium

In June 1957 aged 16 years, my big break came. I re-auditioned and got a place in the John Tiller Girls.

The first of many contracts with the Tiller Girls was for the "Big Show of 1957" at the Blackpool Opera House Theatre. I started rehearsals just before my sixteenth birthday. Top of the bill was Jewell and Warris, two very popular comedians at the time. The producers were George and Alfred Black who were known as the Black Brothers in the theatrical profession. They were very well known for producing spectacular shows and variety. I first had to have my long hair cut. This upset me. I had a hairpiece made out of it so I could pin it back on! I had to choose: keep my hair long or have it cut to be a Tiller Girl.

We had a uniform for rehearsals: white blouse, black pants and black shoes. Our white blouse had a black bow at the neck, and believe me it was a hallmark. You wouldn't dare turn up without it. Height was important too, being able to slot in the line was like saying 'does the shoe fit?'. There were times when we backed-combed our hair to make ourselves taller. You wouldn't get away with it: Miss Barbara would pat it down and make you take your shoes off.

The school rehearsals for Tillers was one week before the company rehearsals, during which time we had shoe and costume fittings.

This training week was in London. Our costumes for this summer season were brand new and made by Alec Shanks. Mr Shanks made the most glamorous, elegant, beautiful, captivating costumes. His designs were exquisite; he was a master of art and sketched the unique designs and colours so we could see the finished costume. Mr Shanks' fitters often used to fit us with just the base or linings so it was always nice for them to show us the finished design Mr Shanks had sketched.

The Black Brothers' show was always spectacular. It ran from June until September. They don't do seasons like that any more. The Tiller Girls were always hired as a speciality act, never as chorus dancers. The Opera House seated 3,500 people. We did two performances per night, six nights a week; a total of 42,000 spectators per week.

While in London rehearsing our Tiller routine, many of the girls got blisters on their heels. You could see some of them in much pain and agony. It was never to stop you carrying on through the pain and discomfort. "Grin and bear it" Miss Barbara used to say, "and whatever happens, smile". It covers a multitude of problems! The blisters were so severe they used to bleed, and a pad of cotton-wool was placed under the blister to try and stop it rubbing on the tender spot. I dabbed surgical spirit on to my blister which was very painful, but one hoped it would quickly dry the blister and harden the skin. This was what my dancing teachers used to do when we got blisters on our toes from doing point work ballet. You were never to give in.

After our week's school rehearsals, Mr Smith arranged our train tickets and travel times, and off we went to Blackpool. I stepped out on that wonderful stage for the first time, looking out to the massive auditorium thinking 'WOW, IT'S HUGE'. It made me feel very lucky. I'd never had a proper holiday or stayed in a seaside before. It was quite an experience just being away from home for weeks and getting paid for it.

A typical rehearsal taken by Miss Barbara showing the correct way of learning our routines.

The next two weeks were our company rehearsals when the show is put together along with the rest of the cast. Most of the first week we finished at around 6 pm. The second week was lighting, costumes, timing quick changes and running the spectacular scenes – in this case, the "Dancing Waters" and "Burning Oil Wells". One of the spectacular scenes the Black Brothers produced at the Opera House was the "Burning Oil Wells" featuring the George Mitchell Singers. Suddenly the oil wells were on fire, flames leapt into the air, smoke and explosions filled the stage when a giant pylon fell crashing to the ground as the curtain fell. Great production!

For the final few days before the show opened, we had full dress rehearsals. In 1957 Rock and Roll was very much in fashion. Jewell and Warris did a scene to close the first half with The Tillers and other members of the cast. As they were singing "We want to rock rock rock, we want to roll roll roll, a pile of rocks fell from the flies over Jimmy Jewel's head; over Ben Warris came the bread rolls. The audience were in stitches. Towards the end of our final week's rehearsals, we sometimes didn't finish until midnight; not one minute over that time otherwise it would have been into overtime pay. Our salary for the company rehearsals was half pay.

On our opening night we received telegrams from both Mr Smith and Miss Barbara and other Tiller troupes performing at other venues in the UK. I also received a special one from my mum and dad which said "You made it love, Good Luck". Today they would be saying "break a leg" and would only be buying a good luck card as telegrams don't exist any more. My parents' telegram made me feel proud and appreciate all they had done for me.

The applause during our Tiller routines was a thunder of appreciation. It was there the moment the curtain went up and it never stopped through each move of formation. At the time, the John Tiller Girls were the most famous dancers in the UK and possibly the world, especially as they were hired for Sunday Night at the London Palladium and performing in the "Crazy Gang Show" in London, Yarmouth, Scarborough, Southsea and Bournemouth; all had Tiller troupes performing.

Towards the end of my season in Blackpool I was offered Sunday Night at the London Palladium TV Series. That was amazing. I felt very honoured and it filled me with much joy and happiness. I couldn't wait to tell my parents. We didn't have a telephone so it took a few days for me to get the good news to them, but you could imagine how excited I was. Me, 16 years old, at the Palladium.

I travelled down to London for my first TV show and stayed at the Theatre Girls Club in Greek Street. It was there I met up with other dancers. The "Leslie Roberts Silhouettes" were rehearsing for the Billy Cotton Band Show for the other channel BBC. In those days they only had two television channels: ATV and BBC, and the television was in black and white. The cameras were huge too, about 2 feet wide and two and a half feet long. They had four of them: one on a trolley moved up and down the centre stalls' gangway which looked like it was on small railway lines, another was placed in the dress circle and a third provided the high overhead shots from the upper circle; the fourth camera was used on stage. Sometimes this was placed in the wings, i.e. on the side, to give profile views of the performers. On other occasions this camera was placed at the back of the stage facing the theatre audience.

At times you were able to see the back of the Tiller Girls looking out over the heads of the orchestra and a moment later you could see our faces, but there was no camera in sight. The explanation for this was that the camera at the back of the stage was always deliberately hidden by scenery. The lens covers the performers through a small opening which cannot be seen from the front of the stage. This was how they got the unusual shots of our Tiller routines.

We had one day's rehearsal on a Friday in a rehearsal room in Camden Town. Our pianist, Pat Dodd, played for us. He was from the original Palladium orchestra and had played for us many times; he knew our tempo off by heart.

Our Tiller routine was set in the morning by Miss Barbara and it was perfect by the afternoon. After lunch the producer, Bill Ward or Albert Lock, would call in to see it and arrange camera shots. Miss Barbara would alter any part of it that needed to be changed, for example, an entrance or exit. We used to finish about 4.30 pm; 4 pm if we were good. Bear in mind, we had been kicking and perfecting the routine from 10.30 am. I don't think a footballer does that kind of training! We would then hobble back to our digs for dinner and a good soak in a hot bath to try and ease our soreness and stiffness and sore feet.

Our next call would be on the Palladium stage by 10.30 am the following morning (Saturday) with our feet sometimes covered in blisters. This rehearsal would be to stage the routine to make sure we had enough room to perform all our formation and for the camera crew to rehearse their shots; our routines were fast moving. We were always finished by lunch time. Sometimes the producers used to like giving us individual close-ups. This annoyed Miss Barbara as the routine wasn't very long due to the time allocated, and the people watching at home would miss half of the routine on screen while the camera was panning along the line of the girls' faces.

On The Big Day - Sunday

At 10 am Val Parnell was in the stalls with his production assistant, Charles Henry, and Miss Wood, his production secretary. Val Parnell was the Head of ATV. His role was to book all the big stars and supporting acts.

The acts would run through their numbers with Musical Director, Cyril Ornadel, and his orchestra or Jack Parnell. The John Tiller Girls were the first act to take their band call; our tempo was most important, slick and fast. It would cause a big impact when the curtain went up. It's amazing how many musical directors played our music far too slow. They used to think they were helping us, but it made it harder. Miss Barbara was always out front to make sure the tempo was right. She would be tapping her hand.

The producers, Albert Lock or Bill Ward, would be directing the cameramen from ATV's blue and white control van parked by the Palladium stage door. There were hundreds of yards of wires and cables. After a break for lunch and everyone had done their band call, more rehearsals followed. Each act was then meticulously timed. Sunday Night at the London Palladium was a live show, you only had one chance. There must be no danger of anyone over-running, and this was the time for cuts to be made.

Lining up for a height check (shoes off no cheating.)

The opening of the show Sunday Night at the London Palladium.

It was the best of times and one of the most thrilling moments of my life. I was in my teens; there was I standing on the London Palladium stage as one of the most famous John Tiller Girls about to perform on television. The clock showed precisely 7.55 pm. I could see the monitor on the side of the stage, it was showing the commercials. The red velvet curtains were down, the lights were blazing on the stage as I began to feel edgy. I kept checking my tights to see if the seams were straight. I could see the girls as they smoothed their elbow-length gloves and made any last minute adjustments to their cleavage and costume.

I shook my head to test my feathered headdress, thinking it's hurting me, it's bound to stay on. We were an exclusive troupe of West End dancers, with a worldwide name, who opened one of the most successful live television shows in British theatrical history 'SUNDAY NIGHT AT THE LONDON PALLADIUM'.

As the Stage Manager counted us down the final five seconds to 8 o'clock, the orchestra struck up "Startime" that famous theme tune. The curtains parted and we were greeted by a wall of sound from the auditorium as 2,500 invited customers cheered at the sight of us. For a few moments we lost the sound of the orchestra and kept counting, hoping we and the musicians came out of the din more or less in the same place. We knew there were another 25 million viewers, a quarter of the UK's population, watching the transmission at home. It was the most deliriously exciting experience I had known.

During the day there had been rehearsals of another sort, an item called "Beat the Clock", for although no-one had any idea who the contestants would be, everything still had to be timed and organised. The compère would run through the various stunts selected with a member of the stage crew and a girl dancer. The

Tiller Girls used to alternate each week with a George Carden or Pam Devies Dancer. I know we used to hate doing "Beat the Clock" and trying out the stunts. While sitting in the stalls watching rehearsals, Miss Barbara would ask two of us to do "Beat the Clock"; we would sink into our seats so she wouldn't ask us. I know then I was very shy but I'd do it willingly now. Two of us did "Beat the Clock" to take the place of the competing couples to make sure the stunts could be done. The format was games created by using different sized balls, hoops or sacks simulated to fairground games or schools' sports days. Two contestants played against the clock, and the couple who completed in the shortest time would win. They would then have to sort out jumbled up words into a well known phrase or saying on a magnetic board. Their prize would be a television, washer or holiday.

Here I am with Bruce Forsyth doing Beat the Clock at rehearsals.

The games you saw played in "Beat the Clock" were worked out by Jim Smith, ATV's Studio Manager. Some came from America where the format "Beat the Clock" had a full hour show, others were worked out by Mr Smith's inventive mind. The couples that competed were chosen from the theatre audience just before the show went on air. The compère would go on stage and ask for volunteers. After tea and biscuits for the artistes in the theatre Palm Court bar, we would do a further run through in full costume at 5 pm.

On my first series of Sunday Night at the London Palladium, Tommy Trinder was compère, but I can remember a short stint of compères: Robert Morley and Norman Vaughan before Bruce Forsyth took over. Tommy Trinder as compère went out over the ATV network on 25 September 1955 with Gracie Fields and Guy Mitchell as the stars. I have a photo taken with David Nixon and Norman Vaughan. I must have been about 17 at the time. Robert Morley, Norman Vaughan and Don Arrol took over for a short while when the resident compère was ill or had other commitments.

Me assisting David Nixon compère Norman Vaughan during a Palladium tv show.

Summer 1958 and I was back in Blackpool at the Opera House with David Whitfield topping the bill. Everyone will remember him for his beautiful voice. Arthur Haynes was also in the show. Although I was a Tiller Girl, we did production numbers as well. That's where the all round dancing comes in. I was also chosen to do a solo routine with Mr Whitfield, before the rest of the girls joined me. I was seventeen years old then. Mum and dad were proud and my dancing teachers were over the moon. Gran and granddad were so excited when during the Palladium TV series I was asked to replace one of the Tiller Girls in 'Crown Jewel' with the Crazy Gang. They were granddad's favourite act, and that was why he had his trips to London every year.

Me, doing my solo dance at the opera house, Blackpool 1958.

I continued doing Sunday Night at the London Palladium TV Shows for quite a few years. My first compère was Robert Morley, then Tommy Trinder, long before Bruce Forsyth and Jimmy Tarbuck. I also did 'Beat the Clock' with Bruce Forsyth. We had fun with that at rehearsals. Sometimes when we did 'Beat the Clock' with Bruce things didn't go right. Bruce would shuffle us along like he does telling us to get a move on. He was always in control and would say "I'm in Charge" which became one of his famous sayings. We did Saturday Spectacular Shows, Billy Cotton Band Shows and Royal Variety Shows. At the beginning of the Palladium TV Show, they were all in black and white. We did the first colour TV for America. I can remember that these shows were the highlight of most people's weekend.

By the 1960s I was doing my third series of Sunday Night at the London Palladium. I had worked on the same bill with Bob Hope, Alma Cogan, Norman Wisdom, Johnnie Ray, Dave King, Nat King Cole, Max Bygraves, David Whitfield, Eartha Kit, Shirley Bassey and Liberace. It's hard to believe that even the Fab Four hadn't yet played at the Palladium. "The Beatles" – by the early 1960s it was Beatlemania, and Val Parnell was getting ready for the big occasion and the screaming girls.

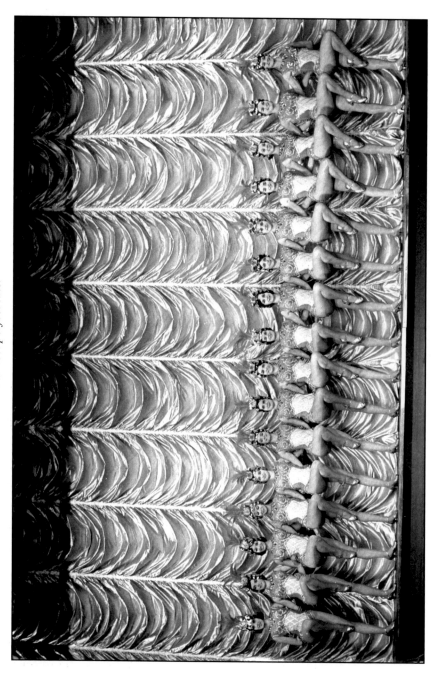

An almost perfect line.

What I recall about the "Beatles" was how clean and presentable they were; all dressed the same and with their bouncy neat haircuts. I didn't pay much attention to their music. I hate it today when acts and artistes walk on in their jeans and trainers. It's almost like they can't be bothered and they have walked on stage or set straight from the street. What's happened to presentation? It can't be the money. We got paid very little in the fifties and sixties: £6 10s 0d for two performances per night; £11 11s 0d for a Palladium TV Show and £2 2s 0d for a costume fitting. These were called guineas in those days.

Before transmission, in every show there was always a long queue outside the little room "The Ladies Powder Room": a line of Tillers in succession wearing their headdresses and dressing gowns, all at the last minute waiting to spend a penny. Nervous, of course we were, and anxious, as we wanted to be successful, worried that one of us would make a mistake and let the whole team down. But we had our Fairy Godmother "DIB DIBS". This Fairy Godmother was invented by the boy scouts. One of the Tiller Girls had this idea that we could have this Fairy Godmother to look after us, and so we did. When finally we were all in costume, we would form a circle and ask our "DIB DIBS" to look after us; make sure there were no mistakes; look after any tricky bits in a routine; make sure the lines were straight and the wheel perfect; make sure our headdresses stayed on. We would also ask DIB DIBS to look after any member of our team if maybe she had a problem with her costume or was in pain from any injury. It always seemed to be right as during transmission you would forget all about it and work through the pain. We used to switch ourselves off from any pain and just go for it.

This brings me to Miss Wendy, my head girl. While we were working in the Five Past Eight Show in Glasgow, she had pulled a muscle quite badly. She went on to do our kicking routine and must have been in agony; she always said she was fine. But that was Wendy. I've never known anyone who has been able to fit into anyone's costume, shoes or hat, but Wendy could. If the shoes were too big by two or three sizes, she used to stuff them with cotton-wool. If they were too small, she would push her feet into them but could hardly walk. You should have seen the look on her face when she said they were fine. She would make us laugh. When she took the shoes off you could see the pain in her face. She would then hobble along the dressing room like Lilly Savage after a few drinks. She was an inspiration to us all, and would never ask us to do anything she wouldn't do herself.

One day when Wendy was taking rehearsals, we were doing the pick-up wheel. On stage, space was very tight. The orchestra was up on a mushroom at the back of the stage. I was on the end of the line and the last to join on, and as the girls came whizzing round I rushed forward to join them. There wasn't enough room and I ended up jumping across the orchestra pit onto the front apron that went round the stage and into the stalls. It was a miracle I didn't end up in the pit or with a serious injury. Although shaken a bit, I saw the funny side and we all had a laugh.

In lots of shows I had a problem with hats. I seemed to have a smaller than average head. To stop my hat falling back, I would have a hair roller in my hair, and on some occasions I would put a 'boob' pad under my hat or headdress. It always did the trick. Some of the headdresses were quite heavy and lots of hairgrips were used. We put that many in our headgear that I used to end up with a headache. I would keep putting more grips in until it made my head 'burn'. That was good because I knew my headdresses wouldn't fall off. I always had a good supply of boob pads to help me out. If they weren't helping to make my bust bigger, they helped to keep my headdress on.

In the early days, we didn't wear tights. We had bare legs for rehearsals and for the shows and TV we had fishnet stockings. They were so uncomfortable. It was a work of art putting them on. You had to pull one stocking up over one cheek of your bum and over the hip of the same leg then tie it round your waist and hip on the other side, then repeat the procedure with the other stocking and leg. You would end up with red lines and blue marks round your waist where you had sometimes stopped your circulation. One of the Tillers lost her stockings during a TV show. She hadn't tied them tight enough, and by the end of the routine they had started to slide down her thighs. Luckily, no-one noticed. These fishnet tights were coarse and had thick seams; they used to make your feet sore. This happened at Her Majesty's Theatre when the show was transferred for one Sunday while the Palladium Theatre was preparing for a new production.

One of the memorable things about Sunday Night at the London Palladium was going round the revolve on the stage during the finale with huge letters spelling out London Palladium. I was one of the taller girls so most of the time I took the end of the line. We only had seconds to grab our letters which we placed in front of us on the revolve. I remember I nearly always had the letter 'M' of Palladium. You had to make sure you had the right letter or the spelling would be wrong.

This weekly presentation of Val Parnell's Sunday night variety show from the stage of the London Palladium had now become an essential part of week-end family life for some 17 million people. No other show on British television had such a regular following. No other programme attracted such a large audience, yet despite the enormous size of the audience, Sunday Night at the London Palladium never lost the intimate touch.

The secret was: each family gathered around its own TV set at home and were made to feel that the show had been specially produced for them. Clever production work and camera shots always managed to capture the famous Palladium "atmosphere", an atmosphere that only exists in the world's number one Music Hall. The whole Show was designed for the personal enjoyment of a few people relaxing before their TV screen.

There has only been, as far as I know, one big breakdown and that was in the early days of ITV when one of the ITV sound transmitters broke down. The crisis happened a few minutes before the Palladium Show was due to go on air. While technicians worked for about 50 minutes at the Crystal Palace to repair the damage and ITV viewers waited by their blank screens, Tommy Trinder kept the Palladium audience entertained. Finally, the Palladium Show reached the screens and Tommy said "Welcome to Monday morning at the Palladium". The theatre audience shouted their applause.

The man behind Sunday Night at the London Palladium was Val Parnell, ATV's Managing Director, who had been in show business most of his life. He was without doubt the last of the great showman's flair. His policy for the Palladium was to make the viewer feel he was one of the audience, and it worked. The bulk of our television audience was in the provinces who never got to a big West End variety theatre, and that's why, once a week, he gave them a seat at the greatest Music Hall in the world.

I read that Val Parnell could tell some wonderful stories about how the public felt about a show by the telephone calls that came through his office. After we (The Tiller Girls) had performed each Sunday, a man would ring Val and ask to speak to one of us; anyone, he wasn't fussy. Val was always polite to his viewers, but after a few weeks this chap was proving tiresome, so with all the severity he could muster up he said for Pete's sake will you stop phoning up every time the Tiller Girls have been on. The chappie, slightly taken aback, said who are you? Val Parnell replied severely, "John Tiller". Val never heard from him again.

We had for many years a "stage door Johnnie" an obsessed fan. His name was George so we called him "Georgie Porgie". He was very keen on one of our girls, and used to send boxes of chocolates round to the stage door. I think he lived in north London and travelled to the West End in his three-wheeled Robin Reliant car. This always created excitement at the Palladium stage door. Over the tannoy the doorman would announce "which one of you wants to collect the chocolates this week" or "whose turn is it this week".

After my first series of Sunday Night at the London Palladium, I found out I had another name. I was going to work in Sweden with the "Tiller Girls" and I needed my birth certificate for my passport. This was my first trip abroad. When mum gave me my birth certificate, I looked at it with amazement. I said "Cynthia" and mum said "yes love, that's your name" with a little smile on her face.

I thought of Hilda Baker and her stooge Cynthia who was very tall, speechless and acted rather dumb. I said to my mum "how come the name Cynthia?". She said when gran was young, she used to visit a travelling road show. There was a girl in the show called Cynthia Layburn. Mum said gran thought she was wonderful and was a great fan of hers. When I was born, she wanted me to be called Cynthia but mum wanted me to be called Fay. Anyway, gran won as on my birth certificate Cynthia got first place and Fay second, so even though Fay was my middle name, my mum called me Fay.

Fay was my name through school, and from the day I was born I was only known as Fay. When I think about it now, what a coincidence it is that I should choose show business as a career. It must have been the destiny my gran put me on.

By 1962 I was doing my fourth series, and in between my Palladium TV series I'd appeared in summer seasons in Scarborough, Bournemouth and Blackpool. The Bournemouth season had Harry Worth topping the bill. He was a funny man with glasses and a trilby hat. He was probably most well known for standing in a shop doorway and lifting one arm and leg out to the side. His TV show started with this stunt.

It was here that the producer of the Billy Cotton Band Show came to see us with a view to doing a series for the BBC. At the end of this Bournemouth summer season, I was offered the Billy Cotton Band Show as Head Girl in the line of Tiller Girls who replaced the Leslie Roberts Silhouettes. I had a nice letter from the producer, Michael Hurl, thanking me for leading such a wonderful line of girls. This was an honour to receive, and we now found our Tiller Girls working for both ATV and the BBC.

THE BRITISH BROADCASTING CORPORATION
HEAD OFFICE: BROADCASTING HOUSE, LONDON, W.1
TELEVISION CENTRE: WOOD LANE, LONDON, W.12
TELEGRAMS: BROADCASTS LONDON TELEX * CABLES: BROADCASTS LONDON-W1 * TELEX: 22182
TELEPHONE: SHEPHERDS BUSH 8000

27 June 1967

Miss Fay Robinson,
Queens Theatre,
<u>Blackpool</u>.

Dear Fay,

    Just a line to say thank you on behalf of Bill and myself for leading such a wonderful line of girls for the first two "Billy Cotton Shows". Everyone at the BBC was impressed by the standard of their dancing, and we will all miss them on the subsequent shows.

    I would be most appreciative if you could convey to all the girls our most grateful thanks for appearing in the shows and also for all their co-operation We look forward to working with them all again in the future.

                      Yours sincerely,

                        Michael

                      (Michael Hurll)
                            Producer -
              "Billy Cotton's Music Hall"

A personal thank you letter from the producer of BBC television Billy Cotton's Music Hall.

Back to the Palladium for another Sunday TV Series. How lucky was I. By the end of 1962 I had appeared on the Palladium stage with star artistes Connie Francis, Marti Wilde, Dave Clark Five, Anthony Newley, Adam Faith, Pat Boone, Cliff Richard and the Shadows, Dickie Valentine, Harry Belafonte, Tommy Cooper, Tommy Steele and Lorne Green from the TV series Bonanza.

Val Parnell's Sunday Night at the London Palladium was 'the world's premier telly-variety production', the show which had chalked up an audience of more than twenty million viewers by 1962. This still stands as the biggest audience for any live TV programme and for any live light entertainment show in this country.

Scene Seven

Working With The Stars

I have worked on TV shows with such stars as Bob Hope, Judy Garland, Johnny Ray, Frankie Vaughan, Hettie King, Shirley Bassey, Vera Lynn and with David Nixon and Norman Vaughan doing a little magic, of which I have a nice photo – and I might add, I'm quite beefy too! It was an honour to have been their assistant for this show. We were in such demand; being the number one troupe, there was plenty of work.

In the late 50s and early 60s we did cabaret at the Savoy Hotel, London, and were paid £11 0s 0d (eleven pounds) per week. After the show we got the 2 am bus from Leicester Square back to our digs in Harringay. In 1960 we made a film for Germany. For one week's filming we received £29 8s 0d (twenty-nine pounds eight shillings). For a single cabaret date at the Dorchester Hotel in Park Lane we would be paid £3 0s 0d (three pounds). I don't know how we used to do it, but we had our digs and expenses to come out of this, and we managed to save. Well I did; I was listening to my granddad and still saving my ten shillings (10s 0d) and a little more by now. I now had the savings bug: the more I earned the more I invested!

Big variety shows included Max Bygraves and 'The Bachelors'. We did these productions by Dick Hurram in between TV work. I worked with Ken Dodd; we did two shows a night and three on a Saturday and all full houses. Tickets were being sold on the black market outside the theatre. The season would run for four months to packed houses. On one occasion Ken Dodd was kidnapped by the university students, and the Tiller Girls rescued him by paying a fee to buy him back. I have the memories, photos, autographs, programmes and some contracts to treasure. I look back on my life and think how lucky I've been. I do think luck plays a big part in one's life.

Working abroad with John Tiller was always safe. We were looked after working in Paris, Germany, Sweden, Spain and South Africa. It was an honour to be asked at twenty-one years of age to be captain (head girl) of a troupe of Tillers in Brighton. My skills picked up from Wendy Clarke came into practice. From here in Brighton I was head girl of a troupe for most of my Tiller years. Duties as head girl consisted of altering the routines, formation, etc. if anyone was off ill, taking a weekly rehearsal as part of ongoing training and paying the girls' wages every week. A letter and report had to be sent to the John Tiller office in London every Sunday. I had to make sure it was in the 4 pm post so it arrived on the desk first thing Monday morning. You couldn't rely on that today with our postal service. Altering the Tiller routines was a skill on its own. The precision and the formations in our routines were very unique.

While doing my Sunday Palladium TV Show, some of the highlights for me included working with Nat King Cole, Sammy Davis, Judy Garland and Gracie Fields. I was in the stalls of the Palladium watching their band calls. Nat King Cole's voice was amazing, I loved it when he sang "When I Fall in Love". Then there was Sammy Davies Jnr. He was one of Bruce Forsyth's favourite performers. He idolised him. Sammy didn't know that Bruce could impersonate him. They did a duet together. I sat in the stalls and watched their band call and thought how well they worked together. You could tell Bruce was so proud to be performing with him. I was overjoyed just to be part of this Sunday night TV show. While watching Sammy Davies tap dancing, I was tapping my feet under the seat in front.

Selection of photos taken with the stars.

Me dancing with Max Bygraves on a Palladium tv show.

With Paul O'Grady after recording for his tv show.

Me with Paul O'Grady and Tiller sister Kath.

Richard Madley, Albert Dock, This Morning programme.

A young Chesney from Corrie

Liz Dawn from Corrie.

Bill Roache from Corrie.

Penelope Keith, Albert Hall, London.

'40 Glorious Years.'
Dora Bryan, Earls Court, London.

David Whitfield and Arthur Haynes, Blackpool, 1958.

Dean Sullivan from Brookside tv show.

Joan Regan at a charity event.

Frankie Vaughan, Palace Theatre, London, 1957.

'40 Glorious Years'
Dame Vera Lynn and Danny La-Rue, Earls Court, London.

Bruce Forsyth Birthday at the Palladium, London.

Eric Idle, Royal Variety Show, Victoria Palace, London.

Watching them rehearse, I noticed how Sammy Davies was so tiny, both in height and build. At times he looked weighed down with his collection of gold jewellery: chunky chains round his neck and wrists and knuckledusters on nearly every finger. He'd been involved in an appalling car accident from which he lost an eye. I suppose this was why he nearly always wore dark glasses. It never affected his performance. He was "Mr Wonderful": a most amazing entertainer, multi-talented, a singer, a musician, a dancer and a comedian.

Gracie Fields was my gran's idol, and when she put her head scarf on and sang "Sally, Sally" I thought of my gran and wished she was still with us.

Some Of Our Experiences

Most of the time on my travels we stayed in theatrical digs, and there were quite a few in those days. They kept names and addresses of landladies at the theatre stage door.

In Blackpool because the season was so long, we had a flat. On the bus going home to our flat one of the girls asked "What's for supper?". I said I didn't know because we had no bread and she said well let's have toast then. On some occasions if we only had one egg left we would have egg dip (that's bread dipped in beaten egg and fried) this meant we could share it. I always knew how to make food go further, having come from a big family.

During my Palladium years most of the time I stayed in digs in Harringay, North London, with a lovely couple. We had done a late cabaret and taken the night bus home in the early hours of the morning. When I put the bedroom light on there were beetles running all over the floor. Some nights I would sleep with the light on, and I remember sharing my bed with one of them. Not very pleasant!

In 1962 during the 'Five Past Eight Show' in Glasgow we rented a house. The weather was very cold. Flowers froze in the vase and we had no water as the pipes were frozen. Again, my experiences came into practice. I emptied the water from the hot water bottle back into the kettle and kept re-using it. One night I slept in nearly all my clothes, and even had a hood on to try and keep warm.

We had a prowler following us while we were there. I was putting the milk bottles out one night by the front door, and as I bent down to place them on the floor these two feet appeared in front of me. I was in such shock I couldn't close the door. I was shaking; I had no strength and was speechless. He said "will you tell the girl in the front bedroom she has a nice back". I reminded the girls to make sure the curtains were drawn properly.

On another occasion abroad in Sweden we were doing the big Outdoor Summer Festival. We had no accommodation and the only hotel was full. They opened a school for us and camp beds were set up in a classroom. It was light nearly all the time. One girl was eating raw carrots under the bed clothes. The sound of the crunching made us laugh and we didn't get any sleep. To make things worse, Miss Barbara had a camp bed in the same classroom so we had to behave ourselves.

In Germany we stayed in apartments. All 16 of us shared a kitchen and one saucepan so you can imagine we had to get on well together. It felt like we were 16 sisters all looking after one another. In Berlin we stopped the traffic! The press wanted a photo in costume - outside. So when the traffic lights turned red, we made a line-up across the road; of course when the lights went to green the car horns were going and the wolf whistles started.

Great stars past and present I have been privileged to worked with.

Freddie Frinton

Billy Dainty

Joseph Locke

Arthor Haynes

MIKE and BERNIE WINTERS
PARLOPHONE RECORDS

DES O'CONNOR
COLUMBIA RECORDS

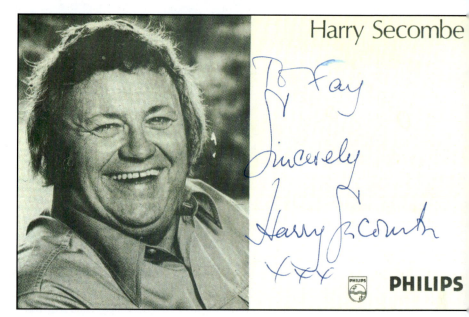

Les Dawson

Ken Dodd

Beryl Grey
(One of the tallest ballerinas)

Bruce Forsyth

Alma Cogan

Sacha Distel

Dickie Valentine

Arthur Askey

Bob Monkhouse

Nat King Cole

While working abroad, this is me swinging my lariat out at sea on an aircraft carrier, HMS Censor.

My Sixteen Sisters

I have many memories of the personalities and distinctive characters of each of my Sixteen Sisters and of some of their mannerisms. To protect their identities, I have given them different names.

Alice was tall and slim. She had a passion for clothes which she carried beautifully on her perfect figure. She loved pay days and off to the shops she would go. We always knew how to keep up-to-date with fashion by looking at what Alice was wearing that week. When sharing digs with her, there was never enough room for hanging your clothes. She said her mum told her never to get rid of your clothes because in the future they will come back into fashion.

Beth was very attractive. She had big dark eyes to match her olive skin which tanned easily in the sun. Some of the girls had the same problem, and would have to tone down their skin colour with a make-up called 'wet white'. The Tiller schools didn't like our skin to be too tanned as it looked obvious next to someone with a very fair skin. They didn't like any strap marks from wearing strappy tops.

Collette was an untidy person. Our space in the dressing room, which we called 'our place', was where we sat and applied our stage make-up. I suppose you could call it a dressing table which had a shelf above to store headdresses. This is where we kept lotions, potions and make-up. Round the huge mirror we would display photos, cards and telegrams from our loved ones. Collette's station always seemed cluttered. How she found her gloves and jewellery among her lotions and make-up beat me. She would throw them in a heap on top of one another.

Some of the girls made pretty covers which were held in place with drawing pins. Mine was pink gingham with pockets on the front for storing gloves, tights and socks. This helped to keep my place tidy. It was Wendy Clarke who gave us the idea, but you had to have some sewing skills.

Della was artistic and very creative. False eyelashes were very expensive. During a long season we would go through quite a few. Della came up with the idea of making them from the black paper that came from a packet of sewing needles. We rolled them round a pencil to curl them.

Elizabeth was a party going girl. We never did find out who she was going out with. She had beautiful skin and told me she never took her make-up off before retiring to bed. Sleeping in her make-up didn't harm her skin.

Fiona was one of our taller girls. She was 5' 8" with fabulous long legs and very small size 4 feet. I said to her "I don't know how you balance with such tiny feet; you would think you'd fall over".

Grace was very pretty with a face that would capture any chocolate box cover. She was blonde, petite and quiet. She never had much to say and would just get on with her work. Her name suited her.

Helen was a very attractive brunette with naturally curly hair which she washed daily. When dressed, she looked immaculate, and could always attract the guys. Her sense of humour was hilarious, and she would have made a good scriptwriter for a comedienne. You could never feel down in the dumps when Helen was around. She would have you laughing in no time at all. Once she was very sick, with her head down the toilet after she had just come in from a party. I said "why do you get yourself in this state", and her reply was "and you think I'm enjoying myself".

Imogen was another Tiller with a great sense of humour. She was tall, dark and very slender. She was very talented, and could play the banjo and put her own words to well-known tunes which were usually about the company in the show.

When Helen and Imogen were together they were a bundle of fun. One morning on stage I was waiting for the girls to form a line-up so I could take our weekly rehearsal. There seemed to be lots of giggling and scuffling going on in the wings. When I asked what was funny, on walked Helen and Imogen in huge Wellington boots. They took their position in line and said "were you waiting for us?". All the other Tillers gave an inarticulate sound of laughter. In this particular show we had the dancing waters, a scene when the waters gave a display of dancing to music. The Wellington boots were left on side stage for two of the crew to put on when checking the water tank.

Jane was one of our quieter girls. She was short in height and had a struggle with her weight. She worked the centre of the line. Her body was short but she had long legs. When we did the stool routine which was choreographed sitting on stools and working our arms and legs, Jane had to have a cushion to sit on to bring her shoulders in line with the others.

Kate had to strive extra hard on her stamina and flexibility. She suffered from stiff joints and tight muscles, especially after a long day's rehearsal. One day she was so stiff and sore she rubbed her aching muscles with a lubrication cream which put warmth and heat into her legs. About an hour after, she felt a burning sensation which was so painful. She couldn't put up with it and ran from the stage to what I thought was the ladies powder room. After a short time when she hadn't returned, I went to investigate. She was in tears in the dressing room sitting in a big white sink full of cold water splashing her legs to keep herself cool. We all saw the funny side, but Kate wasn't amused.

Louise, like many of us in the late 1950s, had a passion for petticoats and full skirts. Tiny waists were in fashion. The more petticoats you wore, the smaller your waist would look. Louise travelled with an extra suitcase for her petticoats.

In London, Wood Green Empire Theatre had the seating in the stalls dismantled so it could be made into a studio for television. This was where we did our Saturday Spectacular Show for television. We did everything in full view of a television audience, including our quick changes. For modesty we wore a flesh coloured body stocking.

Mia, our next in line, always panicked during quick changes. We had costumes, hats, gloves and necklaces all set out ready. Mia, with an overwhelming fear of not making a change in time, grabbed another girl's costume by mistake. It didn't matter whether it was too small or too big, too short or too long, we had to carry on and pretend nothing had happened. You took what was left, shoes and all.

In good times and bad, we all supported each other. We had lots of fun, but we knew when the laughter had to stop. We took our work seriously and would never let one another down. If something did go wrong, we would be so upset and even in tears for letting the rest of our sisters down.

Scene Eight

The History Of Our Mentor John Tiller And Our Schools

I wonder how many women can claim to have been a "John Tiller Girl". It runs into thousands and I'm proud to have been one of them.

Our mentor was John Tiller, a respected member of the Manchester Cotton Exchange in the 1880s. His spare time hobby was amateur theatricals, and he appeared sometimes with the local Minnehand Minstrels. Mr Tiller's pet hate was "ragged" dancing. He dreamed of forming an ideal troupe of his own: his girls, he decided, should be soldier-trained like guardsmen on parade.

It all began in 1886 when he, a successful businessman, who wasn't a dancer but enjoyed music, presented four children from Manchester in pantomime at the Prince of Wales Theatre in Liverpool. In those days they were as young as 10 years old. In fact, I can recall my granddad telling me he was 11 years old when he went down the pit. It wasn't unusual for children to be working by the age of 10 years.

Most Tiller Girls came from the north of our country, not surprising as our mentor, John Tiller, was born in Blackburn on 13 June 1854 the son of Maria Frances Tiller. His father was not known so he was given his mother's surname "TILLER". His uncle, John George, owned one of the largest successful cotton agencies in Manchester and had the most wealthy lifestyle, which his nephew craved. Uncle John George treated John Tiller as his son and took him into the cotton trade. John Tiller worked for his uncle in the day and spent his leisure time singing and writing music. By the age of ten he became a choirboy, and with hard work, later in life, he became choirmaster. His love of music took him to the Royal Northern College of Music.

One day in 1886 John Tiller chose four dancers of identical height and figure. He instructed them that not a leg must rise above a certain line, every head had to turn promptly in one direction and feet must stamp with a sound like a single whip crack. They were to be perfectly drilled and wearing neat short dresses. The girls were launched in Manchester as the "Four Sunbeams".

Maybe it was the precision of the machines that gave him the inspiration and imagination to create a fantasy of patterns, along with the formation that children created in the street playing "ring-a-roses". Seeing the success of his uncle gave him ambition, which was to drive him so hard in life, and his love for music which led him into the theatrical profession. The John Tiller Girls were formed. Most history and information about John Tiller was passed on during conversation with other Tiller Girls and Miss Barbara, our choreographer, who herself was a Tiller Girl. At the age of 19 years he married. They had a number of children, and the first born, a boy, was named after his father and called John Lawrence Tiller.

It wasn't long before the Tiller Girls were dancing all over the world. The Tiller Girls truly were world travellers. The best troupes did number one shows and had bookings in Paris, Vienna, Berlin, Cape Town South Africa, San Francisco, Geneva and America, as well as dancing all over Great Britain and the cinema circuit. Their success was so great that Tiller opened dancing schools and devoted all of his time to training similar troupes. Increasing in number, eventually 48 Tiller Girls became a resident dancing troupe at the Follies Bergère in Paris. It was Tillers "Cocktails", "Sunshines" and "Forget-me-Nots" who first started the continental rage for "Les Girls" as Paris called them.

A further development was child troupes aged between nine and fifteen years. Many recruits came from poor families, and for such children a new world opened. They were fed and cared for. Every "Manchester mite" or "Sunshine Baby" proudly possessed her own little dressing gown, makeup box and initialled suitcase. Out of doors she wore a scarlet hooded cloak, white socks and patent leather shoes. At sixteen she graduated to a senior troupe. Rigid discipline controlled the "Tiller Girls'" travels.

Kindly John Tiller and his second wife, Jennie, were "father and mother" to the 7,500 dancers they distributed around the world during the years of running their schools. Jennie looked after the girls' health and happiness, for being an orphan herself, she realised their need for affection.

It was in 1912 that the Royal approval came to John Tiller when his famous Palace Tiller Girls appeared before King George V and Queen Mary. After watching the Palace Girls, the great Ziegfeld booked a troupe of fifty similar dancers to appear in his famous New York Follies. For this reason Ziegfeld is often wrongly credited with the invention of precision dancing, as it became known. It was John Tiller's inspiration alone.

The troupe of four eventually increased, and by adding more girls: 12, 16 and 20 plus, this gave him more scope and ideas to create better patterns and formation. The cinema circuit and pantomimes gave the Tiller Girls the opportunity to earn their Equity Cards and apprenticeship, after which the best were singled out to go into big shows in London and abroad, and the hardworking successful ones were chosen for television and films.

By now John Tiller was huge in the entertainment profession. His dancers were in big demand, and he was by then opening John Tiller Schools of Dancing in Manchester, Blackpool, London and New York. His son took charge of his Dancing School in Manchester. John Tiller's second wife, Jennie Tiller, ran the school in Blackpool, and all the Tiller Girls had great respect for her. I believe she looked after them all and treated them as her children; so much so, that they all called her 'mother'.

Mary Read was one of John Tiller's most popular, important dancers. It seemed he created a troupe of girls around her, and she worked most of the time in America. It is rumoured she became his mistress. In fact, the United States were booking the Tiller Girls, and he opened a school there. John Tiller put Mary in control of the establishment in New York. It now meant that he was commuting between London and New York, and he was now living an expensive lifestyle which he enjoyed with Mary.

John Tiller died aged 71 in 1925. His wife, Jennie, carried on until her death eleven years later. Characteristically, both Tillers left all their considerable fortune to the staff whose hard work and loyalty had helped found it. In addition to receiving lump sums, twenty of them were named as shareholders in the new firm. Mr Robert Smith with his co-director, Barbara Aitken, ran the John Tiller School in London and business headquarters. Mr Smith, whom I knew, had been over fifty years on its staff. Miss Barbara was proud of the fact that she had never worked for any other management. She began as a small girl in a child troupe and had danced her way round the world by the age of 25.

When Jennie Tiller died it was a very sad occasion for all the Girls. Her memorial service was held in St Martins-in-the-Field, Trafalgar Square, London. It was a very beautiful and deeply impressive farewell as 80 Tiller Girls journeyed all night to attend her funeral on 27 February 1936. After the service she was laid to rest along with her husband, John Tiller, in a grave at Brookwood Cemetery in Surrey. It seems she was the last of the original quartet. In St Stephens-on-the-Cliff Church at North Shore Blackpool there is an Actors Chapel Altar. This was dedicated to the theatrical profession in 1928. A procession of singers, dancers and musicians decorate the marble altar side panels which bear the names of theatrical benefactors. The marble floor is a memorial to Miss Jenny Tiller, founder of our Tiller Girls.

Actors Chapel.
The marble floor with Jennie Tiller's name in remembrance.

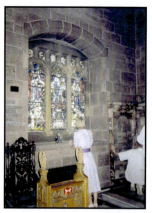

*Actors Chapel.
Me looking at the stained
glass window in memory
of John Tiller.*

The London School was in Charing Cross Road; it was also the headquarters. When I auditioned in 1956 the School was in Old Compton Street, Soho. Robert Smith, known to us as Mr Smith, along with Miss Barbara Aitken our choreographer, and Miss Doris, ran the School in London. It was rumoured that Mr Smith was a relative of John Tiller's first wife. Mr Smith took over the accounts and contracts as mountains of wage packets needed to be done. He also always attended to our travel and train tickets. Wherever we were travelling to, we nearly always had to change at Crewe Station. If you were on tour you would meet up with someone you knew at Crewe Station.

My memories of Mr Smith are of a quiet, stocky, shortish man who seemed to always wear a raincoat and glasses. He was smart and always wore a tie, and I can't recall him ever driving because he always used public transport. He travelled to all our opening nights, and would give us lots of praise for our hard work. In the interval he would send backstage to our dressing room ice creams for all the girls.

I know Miss Barbara travelled by train as she didn't own a car. Miss Barbara was a Tiller Girl herself who had worked for many years for John Tiller and travelled the world. It was always a longstanding Tiller Girl, with obviously much experience, who took the girls and 'Tiller' name forward into the next decade. It was under Miss Barbara's command that I gained all my passion, love and experience for being a Tiller Girl, and of course my mother, whose wishes had come true.

Miss Doris was kept busy in the office typing as she was Mr Smith's secretary. When I auditioned at the office in Old Compton Street - on the top floor - there were no lifts, just a narrow staircase. Miss Barbara took me into a small room which was bursting at the seams with costumes. These costumes were used for cabarets at the Grosvenor Hotel and Dorchester Hotel in Park Lane, London. In that room I changed into my leotard for my audition. I came out of the room to the front of the office which was surrounded by filing cabinets, and I did whatever Miss Barbara asked of me: ballet, tap, modern dance and of course high kicks! The next thing was a measure of height. "Take your shoes off, dear" I can recall her saying and "good, you are 5' 7", and of course that had to be without shoes.

Miss Barbara had a knack of how she chose her girls; she must have known what she was looking for apart from the all-round dancing ability and height. The girls that stayed with Tillers for many years were dedicated, could take discipline and had respect. Miss Barbara was very slim. She would show you what she wanted and would bounce her way through a step when training. Miss Wendy, as she was known, was my head girl for a number of years. I have a lot of respect for her. She taught me lots of skills which helped me tremendously for when I took the role.

Mr Robert Smith and Miss Barbara Aitken ran the School in London and were both directors of the company. In the 1970s they moved from the Greek Street address, and all correspondence was directed to a box number. In the early 1970s Mr Smith was ready to retire and Miss Barbara's health started to deteriorate when along came a "knight in shining armour". He was a wonderful man, Mr Robert Luff, who rescued us and took over The Tiller School and name.

Mr Luff was a tall, slender, courteous, very polite gentleman with a soft gentle voice. He didn't have much hair and always wore a suit and tie, as you would expect from a gentleman. I think it was agreed that Miss Barbara would stay as a director and choreographer, and with the help of Miss Wendy, she was able to carry on.

The late Mr Luff, he was a gentleman.
This picture was taken at the Tiller Girls 'Centenary' 1886-1986, enjoying happy memories, April 1986.

In 1971 things started to go wrong. I was about to do another Sunday Night at the Palladium TV series; this would have been my eleventh. I'd signed my contract for the series and was waiting for my rehearsal call. It was early November and the Palladium series usually started in September. I felt something wasn't quite right. I received a letter from Mr Smith and Miss Barbara with the shocking and alarming news that they both very much regretted to have to tell me that the Palladium Show would not be produced; therefore, they were very sorry they would have to cancel my contract, too.

This came as an horrendous shock and disappointment. I felt my dreams had been shattered. It was devastating! It was to become the start of a big recession for the entertainment industry and the Tiller Girls.

Robert Luff was a theatrical impresario and had been an agent for over 60 years. His clients included Gracie Fields, Beryl Reid, John Pertwee, Lenny Henry and by then the Tiller Girls. His greatest success was as producer of the stage version of the Black and White Minstrel Show which was based on the hugely popular BBC TV series featuring songs from Broadway and Hollywood musicals. It earned a place in the Guinness Book of Records for being seen by more people than any other theatrical production, just as the TV version kept up to 18 million viewers entranced for 20 years (1958-1978) and won the Golden Rose at the first Montreux Television Festival in 1961. It featured the comedians Leslie Crowther, Stan Stennett and Don Maclean.

Two years after its launch on the BBC, Mr Luff, who managed the show's co-creator and conductor George Mitchell (said to have TV's most recognisable back) took the Mitchell Minstrels and the Television Toppers, along with the principal singers Dai Francis, John Boulter and Tony Mercer, on tour in 1962. The show opened at the Victoria Palace, London, where it ran for 10 years with 6,477 performances. Other companies toured Britain, Australia and New Zealand during this time. The stage show continued until 1987; it bounced out with a tour of three Butlins resorts. He owned hotels and theatres in various English seaside resorts where he mounted summer seasons featuring Ken Dodd, Danny La Rue, Frankie Vaughan, Cilla Black and other stars.

The Futurist Theatre, Scarborough, was one of Mr Luff's Theatres. I performed there as a Tiller Girl on a number of occasions. Al

Read, Ronnie Carroll and The Bachelors were topping the bill. We hoped that Mr Luff's taking over of the Tiller School would keep our name going in the variety and entertainment industry.

It was during one of Mr Luff's shows in Scarborough that Ronnie Carroll had arranged a golfing match with some celebrities. Members of the cast from our show, including myself (being head girl at the time), and a few Tiller Girls were invited to have lunch with them. This was used as a big publicity event. One of the top celebrities was Mr Bond himself "James Bond" Sean Connery! I didn't think much of it at the time and just treated it as part of my job to advertise our show, but now I realise what a great honour it was to be asked to be in the company of such a mega great film star.

By the middle of the 1970s, Miss Barbara's health had deteriorated further. She had a severe problem with the circulation in her leg and had two operations to try and save it. Mr Luff gave her some help, and she had daily visits from Miss Wendy and occasional visits from Sylvia Blake, herself a Tiller Girl. Both Wendy and Sylvia were close to Miss Barbara and did a wonderful job looking after her. Miss Wendy would keep us informed of her progress. We were devastated to receive the very sad and disturbing news that she was to have her leg amputated. To think that such a lovely lady with beautiful long legs should lose one of them. It came as an even bigger shock when a few months later Miss Barbara passed away. I couldn't comprehend what went wrong and found it hard to compose myself. It was a frightful shock - what an awful end to her life, someone who had given so much pleasure. It was so very, very sad.

At Miss Barbara's funeral the Tiller Girls had a wreath made like a Tiller Girl in costume. It was about 4 or 5 feet high. I couldn't decide whether I liked it or not; it felt a bit weird and sent shivers up my spine. Nevertheless, the girls chose it and that was good enough for me. It was our way of saying goodbye.

In November 1981 I started to wonder who would continue and carry our mentor's name, John Tiller, forward. I thought "I can do it, I'll do it". I felt I had the experience, the drive and the ambition; it was something I so desired. So I plucked up the courage and put pen to paper and wrote a letter to Mr Luff. I said I could make myself available to help in any way with the choreography and direction of the Tiller Girls if ever required.

I received a very nice letter back to say that unfortunately during the last couple of years, owing to the recession and the consequent problems in the entertainment industry, especially so far as chorus work is concerned, it had not been possible for him to book the Tiller Girls. He said he would retain the name and company and sincerely hoped that it would be possible before too long for a troupe to be seen appearing in first class shows doing the routines for which we had became famous, and he would most certainly bear in mind the interesting fact that I might be available to help in this direction. The letter was signed by Mr Luff himself. I was delighted to receive his reply.

I just didn't want to see the Tiller Girls name disappear after over 100 years. Someone had to keep the name moving forward. Any choreographer can produce a line of girls kicking. Tiller Girls didn't just kick their legs up and do a knee bend, they had a special syllabus that made them unique. You can always tell when another choreographer had attempted to copy a Tiller line. I now just had to wait to fulfil my dream.

Scene Nine

Tragedy, Tears And Laughter

When I was well into my career in show business and dancing at the London Palladium, my sisters, Lesley and Jane, were already taking dancing lessons at our local dancing school in Tickhill. I know mum thought I had done so well she would give them both the same opportunity; after all, they were seeing their big sister performing on television every other week and she was the talk of the village with all the locals.

Factory work or mining was the only work available in the village unless you were very clever. There were not the opportunities for education that the children have today. All I remember was the 11+ which you had to pass to be able to go to college.

My sister, Lesley, was good at tap dancing. She used to have very good beats and rhythm and was really quick at learning routines; she had a very good memory. I recall my dancing school doing a 'Guards Routine'. Lesley was in the troupe and they were working hard for an audition for 'Blue Peter', the children's programme on television. Lesley did not feel well but she would not dare to say anything. She lost consciousness and fell straight back still holding her "gun" (the prop they were working with).

As a small child she suffered from bad headaches. Mum took her to Sheffield Hospital to have electric pads and wires fitted to her head while they did tests on her brain as they thought she was epileptic. I used to think it was because she was very clever. She did very well at school academically, and was quick and bright with figures. She did not take dancing up as a career, which was just as well with all the flashing lights that occurred on stage. She got a very good job working in the office at the bulb factory doing wages and accounts. All her life she suffered from bad headaches. She took paracetamol tablets often.

At a young age, in her 50s, she was diagnosed with a brain tumour which was untreatable, and she passed away far too young. I do believe this problem she had went back to when she was very small. She did marry and have two lovely children, Emma and Martin.

My sister, Jane, did quite well with her dancing, she even auditioned for the John Tiller Girls but fell in love! At the time, she was working at the Crown Hotel, Bawtry, where mum worked. She was waiting on and doing silver service at the big conventions. Mum told me that Tony, the chef, asked her if he could take Jane out. Mum said "yes, if you keep your hands off her". They married very young when Jane was only 18 years old, and to this very day are so in love. It is nice to know that young marriages can work. They have three children: two boys Nathan and Nicholas, and a girl Natalie. Natalie danced for a while and actually performed as one of Ken Dodd's Diddy Men. Jane and Tony went on to run their own catering company and worked as a team most of their lives.

My eldest sister, Anne, who lived with gran and granddad, had a job in Leeds working as a nanny for a well-known store called Schofields. When she was on holiday she would come home with some beautiful clothes which were hand-downs from the children she was looking after. My little sister, Jane, had a beautiful dress with smocking all over the bodice. I loved dressing her up and showing her off wearing these expensive clothes. Anne married the local undertaker in our village.

I was then working in Sweden with the Tiller Girls and did not attend the wedding. Anne had three children, a girl and two boys. Her eldest boy, Joe, was a page boy at my sister Lesley's wedding. I made his outfit, white shirt and deep purple velvet trousers and a bow tie. I also made the bridesmaid dresses.

Joe was a gorgeous little boy, petite, with dark hair and the most beautiful big brown eyes. When he was about 3½ years old he fell off a gate. Tragedy struck one day when my sister was drying him after his bath. She noticed a lump or swelling on his thigh. When she visited mum she brought this to her attention. A visit to the doctors was arranged, then hospital to see a specialist, after which a biopsy confirmed he had cancer. This was hard for us all to take in at the time of someone so young.

We had a long and painful time ahead while he went through awful treatment, losing his lovely hair, with long spells of pain and sickness, weight loss and appetite. I left my little Hillman Imp car with mum; it was not that reliable, a bit of a "banger" really (it was my first motor). She could then drive Joe to hospital so they did not have to take public transport. Sheffield Hospital was quite a journey away. I was then working in London at the Victoria Palace Theatre in the Max Bygraves Show.

At Christmas we always got together as a family, and I looked forward to that time together. It seemed the perfect thing for us to do and we all made the effort, even though I seemed to spend the whole of my Christmas Days washing up. I remember those times with much happiness as a family.

On little Joe's last Christmas, I dressed up as Father Christmas for him. When my sister came to mum's with him, I opened the door and said "ho-ho-ho it's Father Christmas called to see Joe". He laughed and said "Don't be silly, it's Auntie Fay". So much for my acting.

A few weeks passed and my sister was given the tragic news that his cancer had spread. She told mum that she asked the specialist to amputate his leg, thinking this would solve the problem, but she was told it would not make any difference. As a family, this was now hitting us very hard. This had happened just as he had started school. We all thought he was doing so well. A short time went by and he was getting very tired and weak. Anne, my sister, started using a pushchair for him as he could not walk far and he was getting very out of breath.

One day she told mum she was walking through the church yard looking at the gravestones with him. He was asking her to read some of them. One of them happened to be of a young child. He said "Mummy, why did she die not very old?". I suppose as a small child you only associate death with older people. My sister said "Because God only chooses special people" and Joe said "I hope he chooses me".

He was nearly six years old when tragedy struck and he passed away in hospital with us all by his bedside. I never ever want to see another child die this way again. It was a very hard job for his dad to do to make his own son's coffin. Our family was devastated.

My brother, Michael, the third to be born of mum's seven children was different to us. He was diagnosed mentally backward, severely disabled and epileptic. Mum was told he had the brain of a one year old baby. Although he developed normally in other ways, his brain never did. He could not wash or dress himself or hold a conversation. He used to communicate by making noises, and as he grew bigger he could be quite aggressive and strong if he could not get what he wanted. For me, from a young age, I knew our family was different. I began to understand the hardship both my parents endured. I soon learnt a great deal about how to entertain Michael and keep him amused, and how to help mum as much as I could. As a child, I felt by helping mum I got what I wanted (my dancing lessons); for me it felt like a reward for my help.

Michael needed lots of attention and loved his bread and jam and cups of tea. When he was about 18 years old, he was accepted into a mental hospital near Newark where he passed away. My parents had no help from anyone.

My other brothers, Timothy and Jeremy, both worked at the bulb factory where my gran used to pack bulbs into boxes off the conveyor belt on the factory floor. Timothy worked in the offices with my sister, Lesley, and Jeremy's job was directly involved with glass making. Timothy met and married a German lady, Girtie, and went to live in Germany.

A day trip out to the seaside.
My mum, dad, sisters Jane, Lesley, Brothers Tim and baby Jeremy.

Tragedy struck our family again when their first born was discovered to have died late in Girtie's pregnancy. It was tough that she had to give birth normally in a hospital ward where other ladies were having healthy babies. About 12 months later she fell pregnant again, and the good news this time was that she was expecting twins. She had two identical healthy twin boys, Brian and Gilbert.

Jeremy worked very hard and went on to be a control manager for a big glass company in Knottingley; he now does a fair amount of travelling to the EU countries. He met and married Beverley, a special needs teacher, and they have a son, Joseph. Jeremy was the baby of our family and came into the world when I was 18 years old. I remember I was doing pantomime at Golders Green in London. Arthur Askey was topping the bill. I was so proud of having a baby brother. I told Arthur Askey and he sent mum a congratulations card. I was so excited for mum and dad.

My dad with Sam the dog.

When Timothy and Jeremy were young, they would both play tricks on dad. Dad would fall asleep after his dinner and mum would tell him to go to bed if he was tired. On one occasion, the boys brushed Sam the dog and collected the dog hairs and stuffed them in dad's pipe. Dad had left his pipe on a small table at the side of his chair. When he woke he picked up his pipe, lit it and 'BANG'; it was like a firework display. Dad threw his pipe up into the air. Laugh, we could not stop laughing. I will not tell you what dad said! He was a good sport.

On another occasion, usually after the coal had been delivered, there was plenty of coal dust lying around, and sometimes if the fire wasn't lit there was plenty of soot in the fire grate. Once again when dad was asleep, the boys took soot or dust from the coal and drew marks and patterns on dad's face. Dad would wake up and walk into the kitchen to put the kettle on for a cuppa. The boys would be laughing and dad knew they were up to something.

Dad was always game for a laugh. He was a good man, hard working for very little money. A miner's job was dangerous. In those days they didn't have machinery, they were bent double using a pickaxe and sometimes knee deep in water. Dad's job title was a Colliery Underground Tailgate Ripper. Their perks or rewards were a ton of coal which was classed as part of their wages. Dad only had to pay for delivery, which was hard to find at times.

I know mum was delighted that the boys worked hard for alternative careers. She never wanted them to go down the mines. The pit is now closed as well as the bulb factory and the shoe factory. They were the main places for employment in the village of Harworth.

Both my grandparents worked very hard, gran at the bulb factory, granddad down the mines. They saved enough money to sail out of Liverpool on the Empress of England to Toronto Canada. This was a very special occasion for them. It was 1953 and it was the ship's maiden voyage. I have a souvenir book with their names in it, along with all the other passengers making this memorable trip. I was so excited for them. I told all my school friends, and I thought they were very rich. Going to Canada on a boat and not realising how far it was. I thought I must always take granddad's advice and save a little each week when I'm working, which happened to be ten shillings (10s 0d) (equivalent to 50p today) because one day it may make me rich.

Their trip to Canada was to see Aunt Phyllis who they had not seen for a number of years. By now, her family had increased and she had four boys who they had never seen. As the years passed and Freddie Laker introduced Laker Airways, flights became affordable. It made it possible for Aunt Phyllis to come to England more often and we got to know her really well. On one of her visits, she brought one of her sons with her. They wanted to drive to London for a meal and night out – as if it was round the corner! She said they think nothing of driving 200 miles in Canada just for a night out. I said we don't even drive that far for a holiday.

When both my grandparents passed away, my gran in the early 1960s with stomach cancer and granddad in the 1970s with the pit disease emphysema and heart attack, my mum and Aunt Phyllis used to alternate their trips. On Aunt Phyllis' last visit, my sister, Lesley, and I drove to Manchester airport to meet her. The flight was delayed, and after about two hours wait a message came over the tannoy "Could Miss Fay Robinson please go to the information desk". So off I tootled. They never said anything to me, just handed me the phone. It was mum on the phone and she said "you'll have to come home love as Aunt Phyllis had died on the flight over". I could hardly see to drive properly through the tears. I was so pleased I had taken my sister with me for company.

When we arrived home, mum was very upset. She said Uncle Pete had rang her to say Aunt Phyllis had died on the plane, and they had to bring the flight down at Labrador North Canada while they were still in Canadian country. He said she hadn't felt well when she left Toronto and died of a heart attack. It was most upsetting to think she had been on her own. Not long after this, Uncle Pete moved to Ottawa, and I do not know if mum lost his new address, but we lost all contact with our family relatives in Canada.

Scene Ten

By Royal Command

The very first Royal Variety Performance took place on 1 July 1912 at The Palace Theatre in Shaftesbury Avenue in the presence of their Majesties King George V and Queen Mary. Harry Lauder, a singer, and Anna Pavlova, the Russian ballet dancer, were top of the bill with Vesta Tilley and Little Tich.

The Royal Variety Performance is a charitable event; the funds go to the Entertainment Artistes' Benevolent Fund. It is both an honour and of great pride to be asked to perform in such a show. It raises thousands of pounds for the upkeep of our residential home, Brinsworth House in Twickenham. This helps thousands of performers in the variety entertainment industry, young and old.

The famous John Tiller Girls made their debut in the Royal Variety Performance on 27 May 1926 at the Alhambra Theatre London with a line up of twelve girls. The Press had picked up that it was notable that the new comers of 1926 were the Tiller Girls and the comedian/singer Dick Henderson, the father of the late star Dickie Henderson.

On 11 May 1931 at the Palladium the John Tiller Girls performed in the presence of their Majesties King George V and Queen Mary. It was at this performance that John Tiller brought together three troupes of Tillers: the twenty-four Mangan Tiller Girls, twelve Carlton Tiller Girls and twelve Plaza Tiller Girls made a total of forty-eight in the line-up. I can imagine the spectacular formation this must have created. I often wondered where the Changing of the Guards got their ideas from.

Also in the show were a further sixteen Sherman Fisher Dancers and the Palladium Dancers. Topping the bill was the 'cheeky chappie' Max Miller. The John Tiller Girls is probably the only line of dancers ever to appear before royalty for *"eighty-six years"*; that must be a world record. How proud to think our John Tiller Girls' name has performed for more generations of royalty than any other star name worldwide.

I was extremely honoured to be asked to appear in the 1964 Royal Variety Performance as part of the John Tiller Girls line-up. This took place on 2 November 1964 at the London Palladium in the presence of Her Majesty Queen Elizabeth II. It was presented by Bernard Delfont and produced by Robert Nesbitt and had the most fantastic star line-up. Humour came from Morecambe and Wise and the irrepressible Tommy Cooper, with a young rising star from Liverpool, Jimmy Tarbuck, whose humour captivated the audience.

Many people were seeing him for the first time. He had worked with us previously where he had a small billing. It was this show that made him a household name. Also on the bill was a group of lady singers: Cilla Black, Millicent Martin, Kathy Kirby, Brenda Lee and the fabulous Gracie Fields (my gran's favourite). The Bachelors sang "I Wouldn't Trade You for the World" to the Queen in the Royal Box to spontaneous applause from the audience.

On stage at the Palladium. I'm on the end of the line on the right.

There was a problem with the Tiller Girls' black velvet costumes. They had gone missing, eventually to be found in the gents' cloakroom. An embarrassed worker at the Palladium dismissed the event too defensively. We didn't really think there was anything sinister about the incident. It was probably some sort of misunderstanding. I was not convinced. Thank goodness it didn't happen on the night, it was unnerving enough. It did make me realise why the Tiller Girls always wore a uniform for rehearsal. Miss Barbara used to say if ever anything goes wrong with our costumes, being in uniform we could always perform. On this occasion it almost did.

With Cliff Richard and the Shadows topping the bill, it was one of the greatest, most wonderful days of my life. To a performer, a Royal Variety Performance is the highest accolade and certainly the most nerve-wracking he or she will ever tackle. As a solo performer, if you make a mistake you would be letting yourself down, but being in the line of Tillers, you would be letting the other fifteen down. This show was special for me as it was my first performance before royalty. I was head girl which made it a "winning line", and both my parents and family were able to see me perform on this most wonderful occasion.

Being in the company of the Royal Family was beginning to be a habit for me as you will see when you read further into my life story.

THE LONDON PALLADIUM

Monday, November 2nd, 1964

Bernard Delfont, Leslie A. MacDonnell O.B.E., & Arthur Scott

tender their congratulations to

Fay Robison

on being selected to appear before

HER MAJESTY THE QUEEN

and

H.R.H. THE DUKE OF EDINBURGH

on the occasion of the

ROYAL VARIETY PERFORMANCE

in aid of the

The Variety Artistes' Benevolent Fund

Scene Eleven

Changing Direction

In November 1971 after receiving the most dreadful news that our contract for the new Palladium series was to be cancelled, Mr Smith and Miss Barbara had suggested we try something else. I felt sick from the stomach; a mad panic came over me; it was a big blow to my career; a feeling that the bottom had come out of the boat and I was sinking. After all, dancing was the only thing I had done. I didn't want to end up working on the factory floor, not after all the work and effort mum and dad had done for me. I wanted to prove I could do better, even though I didn't do well with my school education. I wanted to be somebody notable, a household name or public figure, and I was prepared to work for it. The name 'John Tiller Girls' gave me that feeling, it hit hard to be told there was no work.

My first reaction was to buy "The Stage" - a weekly newspaper especially for the entertainment industry. Dancers, actors, performers, musicians and stage technicians all purchased this when looking for work. This came out on a Thursday. Dancers used to pick it up and over a coffee would scrutinise, study and scan the back few pages where jobs would be advertised.

I spotted one for dancers for the "Starlight Room" in Blackpool at the Winter Gardens Ballroom. It was for Billy Petch Dancers. They were looking for 12 girls, and the audition was at The Talk of the Town in London. One had to be in full make-up, high-heeled shoes, leotard and 5' 7" tall. Before we even had the chance to dance, we had to stand in front of Mr Petch and company, front view, side view and back. I thought I hope my bum doesn't look too big and my legs look longer. For my height, I had quite short legs. After passing the first part of the audition, I went on to dance. I was one of the lucky ones and off I went to Blackpool.

Me trying to be a model to keep myself in work between contracts.

The Starlight Room was a once nightly Cabaret Show and the costumes were very glamorous. After our show, from 11 pm until 1 am in the morning, Joe Loss and his orchestra would play in the ballroom for public dancing. This famous bandleader was very well-known for his dance music and personality. He was small, petite, had lots of energy, and he would jump up and down with his baton while conducting his band.

Life for me away from the Tiller Girls was a new experience for which I was grateful, but I missed my Tiller friends and "family". It also meant that in between contracts I had to find other work which was usually doing promotions or the dreaded 'double glazing', would you believe! I was once offered a job as a petrol pump attendant by the dole office. This was so I could keep my stamps on my card for my national health insurance.

The following summer I had a telegram from Dick Hurran, along with Robert Nesbitt: they were the greatest producers of spectacular shows. I had worked on many occasions as a Tiller Girl in his productions, and Mr Hurran asked me to phone him at the Prince of Wales Theatre in London if I would like to do The Opera House Blackpool for the summer. That turned out to be a good move for me because he also offered me the position of Assistant Choreographer, and of course that gave me more pennies. With the extra fee, I bought myself a Rotary white gold watch.

Winter Gardens Ballroom Cabaret.
Me appearing with the Joe Loss Band.

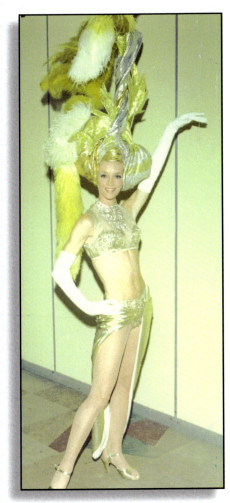

In the mid-1970s I saw an audition in the Stage paper for dancers for a new theatre restaurant in Birmingham. The idea came from Robert Nesbitt who worked with Bernard Delfont. Mr Nesbitt had previously turned the London Hippodrome Theatre, which is situated in Leicester Square, into a theatre/nightclub/restaurant called the "Talk of the Town" and he wanted to do the same in Birmingham. The club was able to seat about 800 people with the theatre stalls converted into a spacious area with dining tables. The centre would house a raised stage complete with orchestra for the star cabaret, and it would then be lowered for the audience to dance on. There would be more dining space up in the dress circle. It was an idea that went on to be a tremendous success for many years and the stars loved performing there.

The "Night Out" was more or less based on the "Talk of the Town". It was to be something very big and new for Birmingham. The difference was it was a purpose-built building, not a converted theatre like the "Talk of the Town", and was much bigger, seating 1,200 people. The seats were in lilac, blue and purple and looked very glamorous. There were lots of girls at this audition. I suppose being outside London, it was a stable contract to get, and would give dancers a bit of security knowing they would be signed up for a few weeks.

I was 34 by then, and knew I had to work hard to keep up with the younger girls. Luck and experience was in my favour and I was offered the contract; it was for 56 weeks. How wonderful and a great surprise to be chosen to be head girl, which made me feel very proud and gave me my confidence back.

Sir Charles Forte and Bernard Delfont formed a partnership, Sir Charles being the owner/manager of the huge chain of hotels and caterers. The "Night Out" Birmingham became Entam Leisure Ltd. My stay at the "Night Out" went on for a further six years where Mr David Wiseman and Miss Jean Clarke produced, directed and choreographed the wonderful, glamorous productions which changed every year. Some of our costumes came from the "Talk of the Town" London. I would always scavenge in the skip for a costume with the name Rosalie on the label as I knew this had been worn by my Tiller friend Rosalie. The costumes were made so well so with a little titivating we managed to get a further season from them, then with clever lighting they would always look like new.

Birmingham 'Night Out'
At my fittest and enjoying
my time there.

The "Night Out" gave us lots of opportunities for extra work. Companies would take over the building and we would do trade shows and private conventions.

In mid-1975 I was very privileged and honoured to attend the opening of the NEC National Exhibition Centre. I was invited along with another dancer to welcome her Majesty the Queen at the opening ceremony. I have a wonderful photograph of this occasion taken with the Queen, one of many with the Royal Family which I will always treasure.

Opening the N.E.C in Birmingham.
Meeting her Majesty, The Queen.

Other members of the Royal Family.

During my stay in Birmingham, I lived with Mr and Mrs Clancy, an Irish family of whom I became very fond. They lived in a big house in Moseley, and I rented the top floor flat. They were very kind to me and would invite me down for Sunday lunch. I felt like one of their family. They always made my family welcome when they came to visit and see me at the "Night Out". Mum came with Auntie Phyllis when she was on one of her visits from Canada. I had a little mini car at the time, and when I went home to Yorkshire to pick them up, my drive back to Birmingham was a nightmare. It was pouring with rain, and trying to get the luggage in my little car with two passengers and myself was a work of art. Aunt Phyllis was amused and laughing; she said that back home in Canada they could almost get my mini inside their American car boot. I didn't think she felt safe in such a small car.

I drove home quite frequently from Birmingham. Dad came back with me to see the cricket at Edgbaston when he took a few days holiday. He used to love watching the cricket and listening to the Grimthorpe Colliery Band. Apart from an occasional trip to Blackpool, I guess that's about as far as he travelled. He had never been abroad, never experienced flying, always travelling by coach or train, and always on his own. It was obvious to me that mum and dad never holidayed together or we as a family. It was always mum that came to see me with one or two of my brothers or sisters or dad on his own. I often wondered why but wouldn't embarrass them or myself by asking the question. I did think that maybe one of them had to be at home to care for my severely handicapped brother, Michael, or it could have been because they couldn't afford it. I think it may have been the latter, but I will never know! Although, if mum was short of cash and needed a bit of help, she would ask me. This she did on the odd occasion if dad had been off work ill, and it was usually to pay the rent.

Dad was a quiet man and shy and never ever asked me for anything. Knowing what he went through health-wise during his short life, I wished he had. We spend our lives saying to ourselves "if only" and "I wish", but by then it's always too late.

In 1980 dad became quite ill. He was a very slim man even though he had a huge appetite. He could eat for England! Mum would cook Yorkshire pudding with our dinner everyday. Dad would always have extra Yorkshire with jam on afterwards as if it was his pudding. We used to think he had hollow legs as he never put weight on. We didn't realise that he must have been ill for a number of years.

About four weeks before dad passed away he was missing shifts at work. He must have been feeling pretty grotty. In those four weeks he kept having bad nose bleeds during which time he had made a couple of visits to his GP. I had been home for the weekend and was getting ready for my drive back to Birmingham on the Monday. Dad came out to wave me off as usual. I gave him a kiss. He didn't look very well, and I told him to go back to the doctors. As I drove off, I turned my head and blew him another kiss; he just stood and waved until I had gone out of sight. I sensed something wasn't quite right; he looked very down, drawn and pale.

On the Thursday of that week, dad had a really bad nose bleed, and off he went to the doctors who immediately sent him to the hospital to have it treated. They did tests and the following day, Friday, mum got the dreaded news that he had terminal cancer. I was taking a rehearsal that Friday at the "Night Out" when my brother-in-law rang to give me the sad news. With my eyes full of tears and mascara running down my cheeks, I said I would go home to see him the following day, Saturday.

That day never came because that morning I received another call to say he had passed away. I was in shock. I couldn't believe the quickness from dad walking into hospital and him dying less than two days later. All I could think about was him waving to me until I'd gone out of sight when I was driving back to Birmingham. I thought we would have him for a few more weeks after him being diagnosed with this terrible disease. I was thinking what we could do for him for what little time he had left, but he didn't have any. I felt much hurt inside me that he was taken from us so young. It was too late beating myself up inside and wishing what I could and should have done. Things were just starting to get better for us.

Before dad died, mum, dad and myself were planning on buying our council house. We had been talking about it for a few weeks. Dad passing away made things more complicated as mum was upset and worried she would have to leave our home for a smaller place. The council would want her to move from our bigger house now the family had all left home as there was only mum and me. The council had built only about six four-bedroomed houses in the village, and mum had one of them. So we sat down with a nice cuppa and did our sums. Mum wasn't working then; she was a pensioner. She feared they would expect her to move into a council bungalow, but because of her age she wouldn't get a mortgage, and even I was getting on a bit by then for a mortgage.

I wanted mum to be happy. She wanted to stay in our family home, and the only way was to buy it. So mum and I bought it together. She gave me her half of the mortgage out of her state pension every month. We purchased it together and it was in joint names. This meant we had a home that mum was happy and settled in and I had a home to go to if I was in between contracts. I would have liked to have bought the house myself, but I was already paying for my accommodation wherever I was working. I looked at this as an investment. I suppose it was the best place to put my money "in bricks and mortar".

In the early 1980s the "Night Out" closed as a big cabaret and entertainment venue. Star names and dancers, including myself, found ourselves looking for work once again. The "Talk of the Town" in London had also closed. That opened up as "Stringfellows Night Club", and I believe the "Night Out" Birmingham became a disco nightclub. So both venues lost their glamorous cabarets and spectacular productions. Work for dancers was becoming very scarce and scanty. There were insufficient jobs now available in the variety field, and it was now time to consider which direction to go. I still had the fear of letting my parents down.

I knew I had to find work. Mum couldn't afford to keep me and I certainly didn't expect her to. I found myself back buying the Stage paper where I scoured and searched thoroughly and energetically through the job section again. In the meantime, I worked doing in-store promotions, double glazing and as an Avon representative. I worked in the Co-op store in Retford for a double glazing company "Horizon Windows". They let me down badly. It wasn't an easy job and I hated it. I did two weeks there for them, travelling 200 miles, and they went bankrupt. Of course, that meant there was no wages for me at the end of my two weeks work.

Then, in the job section of the "The Stage" I saw an advertisement for "Lionel Blair Aerobics". He wanted dancers to teach aerobics fitness classes. I went down to London for my interview and was offered the job for my area, Doncaster. It was first run as a franchise where a fee was required. The company provided training, portable cassette players, stationery, routines and tapes, and they would take a percentage from the takings each week. It was your job to teach and find the venues, as many as you were prepared to do, but with a minimum. We were running this under Lionel Blair's name but we never saw Lionel Blair. Then the company decided to fold-up.

We were told we could carry on with our business which we had built up but to withdraw using Lionel's name and all stationery. I continued running these classes for a few months then numbers were beginning to tumble. I found after deducting my expenses from my takings, I wasn't making much at all. The only good thing was, I was living at home with mum which I hadn't done for years. It was so nice to have home comforts.

I gave up my fitness classes and went to work for Ronnie De-Vere at the Wakefield Theatre Club; it was a short contract and we were called the Ronnie De-Vere Dancers. There were only four of us. The good thing was, I could still work from home, even though it involved a lot more travelling. This short contract at the

Wakefield Theatre Club wasn't renewed, but it kept me going for a few weeks. It was a lovely venue to work, and I was sorry when it came to an end. It was a venue similar to the Talk of the Town in London and had a big star name topping the bill each week.

I went back to my local dancing school and helped with the children. I hired a room and took ladies exercise classes. By then, fitness started to boom. On a visit to one of my Tiller Girl friends, Rosalie, I was looking at the job section of the local newspaper. I saw an advertisement for a gym and fitness instructor at Jean Graham's Health Club in Wallasey. I thought "is this the time to change direction and try for the fitness industry". I applied for the job, and a few days later I got a phone call with some very good news.

Mr Richard Birchall who managed the health club rang me to thank me for my letter, and said he would like to meet up with me for a further interview. I said I would be delighted. When I asked where, when and what time, as I had a 120 mile drive, Mr Birchall said he was prepared to travel to see me, and arranged my interview over lunch at a nice hotel in my home town of Doncaster. When I put the phone down, I thought this is the time to change direction if I was lucky enough to be offered the position. It would give me the security I needed. I was now in my 40s with a mortgage, and deep down I knew a dancer's career was short-lived. It was now 1984. The only worry I had was I would be leaving mum on her own. I had hoped she hadn't got too used to me being at home.

After my interview with Mr Birchall, where we discussed my career and previous experiences and the background of his family business, I was offered the job. I was 'over the moon'. It was a new venture and career for me; I felt it was a new beginning, and I couldn't wait to dig my heels in and make it successful. It meant

I now had a full time job, a wage every week and I could plan my future. I craved the nice things in life and I wanted a better standard of living, both for myself and my mum. Most of my life my work had been on short contracts, so it gave me a nice feeling to think I now had a proper job. This position was working for a ladies only health club.

I loved working with people, helping them achieve results and look their best. I knew I would work full out at this job as I, too, had a passion for health, fitness and beauty, and I wanted this to rub off on the gym members and other members of staff. My first priority was to be the best I could be at my job. I wanted to gain more knowledge and qualifications, both in fitness and the gym. Mr Birchall never let anything stand in my way, and whatever I needed or wanted to benefit the health club, he would go along with. I gained qualifications in weight training with my NABBA (National Amateur Body Building Association), RSA (Royal Society of Arts) Exercise to Music, Diet and Nutrition. I studied hard (it was like being back at school) and became an RSA Assessor and passed my City and Guilds Assessors Award.

These certificates meant I could now examine at an RSA teachers exam. It played a huge part in training. Students wanted to be fitness instructors, and Jean Graham's Health Club became the first health club on the Wirral to introduce Step Reebok Classes, which is still very popular today. Callanetics was another class which had members queuing to get into the studio. This class suited all ladies whatever level of fitness and age, and proved to produce considerable inch loss and tone. It became a challenge for our members. Weight loss wasn't important, as with all exercise, to gain lean tissue meant one could actually gain weight. It was the tape measure and dress size that showed the results!

I was taking about 18 to 20 classes per week. The club class timetable no other club in the area could compete with, and the buzz in the club was tremendous. It was booming and so was the fitness industry. Our slimming group classes were showing excellent results. They had an eating plan to follow, along with exercise classes to suit everyone's health and lifestyle. It was good to know that female fat-cells are physiologically different from male fat-cells. I used to explain that they are smart, stubborn, love to store fat and hate to give it up. The world's leading obesity researchers have discovered that a woman's fat-cell is bigger because it has more fat storing enzymes, while a man's fat-cell is smaller because it has more fat-releasing enzymes. Oestrogen feeds the fat-cells of a woman's hips, buttocks and thighs. It protects the fat-cell by making it extremely efficient at storing fat. This explains the increase in body fat during puberty, pregnancy and when a woman is taking oral contraceptives oestrogen replacement. As soon as fat-cells realise that calories have been reduced, they throw a "party" and invite the lipogenic enzymes to store fat. Dieting simply increases the size of a fat-cell and improves your body's ability to store fat. So my advice to all women is NEVER DIET, follow a healthy eating plan and exercise. The two go together, and changes have to be made as we age. Eat to live, don't live to eat. Exercise to keep the body moving.

During my early years at the health club, we lost one of our most famous comedy double act duos, Eric Morecambe. It came as a big shock to the entertainment industry. I saw an advertisement in The Stage for an audition for "Tiller Girls" to perform in a big television show at the Palladium for a tribute to Eric Morecambe. My first reaction was that I would love to do that. When I told mum she said "you are now in your 40s love, there will be lots of young dancers there". She was thinking how upset I would be if I went down to London and didn't get it. I was thinking, if I don't go, I would never know and perhaps I might be lucky. I found myself on the train going down to London, a bit apprehensive and nervous, even though I was much experienced, but I was in fear of being rejected. One never knows what one is looking for.

I was put through exactly the same as all the other dancers, and at the end of a gruelling day, I was asked to step forward. My heart was thumping. Other dancers were put in line with me and my heart was pumping harder. Were they going to say "thank you very much, you can go" or "you are the chosen line"? Yes, I made it! I was one of the chosen 16 girls to perform in the Eric Morecambe tribute. I couldn't wait to phone mum and tell her the good news. My journey back home was a lot more pleasant.

During rehearsals for this special TV show, I was asked to step forward. The rest of the dancers were told that as I had a wealth of experience, I would be head dancer for the duration of the show. I also helped with the direction and choreography. We did the "Pony" routine during our exit and applause. We were dressed as ponies. Our outfits were very elaborate and realistic with beautiful white tails and plumes from a detailed horse's headdress. We entered the stage with four sets of four girls with each set having a lady driver holding the reins attached to our costume. The driver held a whip which they gave a signal with, then we would change direction or form another formation. We came back on stage and across to the other side, then Angela Rippon joined on to me at the end of the line. I don't know whether the tremendous applause was for us or her! I would hope it was for us. She was dressed as a Tiller Girl in the same costume as we were. To do this show, Mr Birchall gave me leave as he did on a number of occasions.

Scene Twelve

1960s Tiller Girls Reformed Performing For Royalty

In 1988 George May, a choreographer, was asked to choreograph the Christmas Show "Joy to the World" which was to be televised from the Albert Hall in London. He was a close friend of Sandra and Roy Jones. Sandra was one of our original 60s Tiller Girls, and during conversation with George May, it was mentioned that one of the themes of the show was going to be the song "Twelve Days of Christmas". Sandra said she could probably get together eight 60s Tiller Girls, with herself making nine, to represent the nine maidens dancing. This turned out to be a nice feature for the show, and the 60s Tiller Girls were reformed. So it's our thanks to Sandra for starting the ball rolling for many shows that followed.

Roy, Sandra's husband, went into film directing in 1989 and became very busy working on films. Bruce Vincent came to our rescue and took over the bookings and running of our mega-marathon charity events that followed. I don't know whether he knew what he had let himself in for. He did a wonderful job keeping us all together, and I know we would all like to say a big 'Thank You' to him, and to Sandra and Roy, for bringing us together.

The next big show for me was in April 1989 "The Terry Thomas Benefit Gala". This was at the Theatre Royal Drury Lane for the Parkinson's Disease Society. Terry Thomas was suffering from this terrible illness, and his friends and many artistes in the entertainment industry got together to raise funds for this very famous actor. He will be remembered for his posh voice and puffing a cigarette in a cigarette holder. It was from this show that we were so well received and booked as the 1960s Tiller Girls. It was with the kind permission of Mr Robert Luff to use the Tiller Girls name and much help from Mr Bruce Vincent that the 1960s Tiller Girls were reformed. When asked by Bruce if I could make myself available, I didn't need asking twice! My beating heart of the travelling, the theatrical world, the smell of the grease paint, the heat from the footlights and the thrill and excitement of the applause that the Tiller Girls gave me – I couldn't say no.

From them on, all the shows were done for charity. All my performances I managed to fit in during my full time work at the health club. I chose to take them as my holidays, although some I did at week-ends. It gave me much pleasure to do something I enjoyed for charity.

1960s Tiller Girls.
We are back performing our many charity events.

Are they ready for us yet?
At the Palladium.

TILLER GIRLS COME TRIPPING BACK INTO THE LIMELIGHT AFTER 30 YEARS

OH, HOW WE DANCED: The Tiller Girls of the 1960s go through their high-kicking routine, one of the highlights of Sunday Night at the London Palladium

Alive and kicking

FEATHERED FRIENDS: The Tiller Girls at a celebrity gala in Buxton

THE high kicks do not come as easy as they did 30 years ago, but the applause at the end of the five-minute performance says it all: The Tiller Girls are back.

With a combined age of more than 800 years, 16 of the Sixties Tiller Girls have teamed up again and are in constant demand for charity shows all over the country.

The squad includes Fay Robinson from New Brighton, Kath Darragh and Rosalie Kirkman from Wallasey — friends since they were five — and Hazel Maxfield who lives in Skipton, West Yorks.

Kath, who ran her own fitness centre until retiring two years ago, explained: "We were always one big happy family when we danced in the Sixties. We were like sisters and always kept in touch.

"The revival came when a choreographer wanted Nine Ladies Dancing for a Christmas show at the Royal Albert Hall. He approached one of the original Tillers to get a team together and the four of us from the North joined up straight away.

"Then we thought it would it be marvellous if we could get the whole troupe together — and we've never looked back."

Fay, who runs three gym schools in New Brighton, said: "From a distance we still look good and it's only when we get closer to the camera that people realise we are not as young as we used to be."

Hazel, who owns and works in a shoe shop in Skipton, said: "We get the chance to meet up again, have a laugh, a natter, and a party. It's also a good way of keeping in shape."

They admit they are not quite as energetic as they were 30 years ago but their routine is still as precise and regimented.

"We only perform for five minutes," said Rosalie. "It was gruelling when we were in tip-top shape, so it's doubly hard now and there are a few red faces at the end.

"We all keep fairly fit by exercising, but I'm not as keen as the other three. I tend to cram all my workouts into a few days before a show and then wish I had been more dedicated."

The stage wear is kept in immaculate condition by June Vincent and her husband Bruce, who live in the South and meet the girls at the venues armed with six huge wooden crates of sequinned costumes, top hats and feather head-dresses.

■ Accomplished musician John Tiller founded the Tiller Girls more than 100 years ago as a pantomime chorus for the Liverpool Empire.

They reached the pinnacle of their fame in the Sixties when they were a highlight of Sunday Night at the London Palladium.

KNEES UP: Kath, Rosalie, Fay and Hazel show a leg

By PAM MARSDEN

1960s Tiller Girls.
We are back performing our
many charity events.

One or two stand out in my mind. In 1990 there was the "Lerona's Celebrity Spectacular" at the London Palladium for the Spinal Research Trust in the presence of the Princess of Wales. In more ways than one, this was a special occasion for me having the opportunity to meet Diana Princess of Wales. She was a charming glamorous young lady who had a great interest in dance, and she was amazed at our performance and stamina.

In 1992 there was "The Great Event – Forty Glorious Years of our Queen" for the Royal Anniversary Trust. This was a huge spectacular and special occasion held at Earls Court in London. It was so special as the whole of the Royal Family were present except the Princess Royal and Her Majesty The Queen Mother. It was at this occasion that everyone was beginning to notice how unhappy Princess Diana was looking. The Star line-up was mega. There was Darcey Bussell, Petula Clark, Cilla Black, Michael Ball, Dame Judi Dench, Lonnie Donegan, Cliff Richard, Danny La Rue and Dame Vera Lynn, with the regimental bands pipes and drums, Horse Guards, Grenadier Guards, Coldstream Guards, Scotts Guards, Irish Guards, Welsh Guards, The Kings Troup and Royal Horse Artillery all filling the arena. The excitement was endless. The Nation paid tribute.

Here we are opening the great event 'Forty Glorious Years of our Queen.'

Then on came the beautiful Gold State Coach used by The Queen for the Coronation in 1953 and the Silver Jubilee in 1977. What a great memory from when I was a little girl watching this coach on our black and white television screen in our 'Hut for a Home' for her Coronation. Back stage we were very honoured to be allowed to photograph this most beautiful of coaches; it was like a fairytale come true. The great arena had been built such as never seen before. Guests sat in great comfort with a perfect view of the enormous stage, upon which a cast of five thousand artistes performed while the Royal Party and invited guests watched "Forty Glorious Years" unfold. What a great honour and such pride to have been part of this most memorable event; it made me feel proud to be British and how wonderful to have our Royalty.

After our big finale, the Royal Family came back stage where I was introduced to Prince Edward. Would you believe it, there was a picture of him taken by the press with me stood by him which even made it into "Hello" magazine! I have wonderful memories of this occasion and photos taken with Dame Vera Lynn and Danny La Rue. It was from this photograph of me with Prince Edward that Mr Richard Birchall put together a competition for the Health Club members. It read "The Prince and the Showgirl", and the members had to fill in a caption of what Prince Edward was thinking. Some of the comments were quite amusing, and although a dancer never liked to be called a showgirl, I overlooked it on this occasion. A dancer was a dancer, a showgirl was a girl showing off her beautiful costumes. The caption that won was "Quick call Dudley Moore, I've found the chickens". The winner was decided by the votes of a panel of twelve club members.

As mentioned earlier in my story, the 1960s Tiller Girls had now reformed under the direction of Miss Wendy Clarke and Mr Bruce Vincent. Without these two, and of course Sandra and Ray and permission from Mr Luff to use the Tiller name, our charity shows may not have taken place. It is fair to say that most of our 60s line-up are now aged 65 to 75 years old. Nevertheless, our 20 years of charitable events still give us our moments of glory, all for good causes, and a list of events up to date can be seen on page 154-166 of which we have done over 160 shows and raised thousands of pounds for charity.

Meeting royalty after the great event.

All charity events for good causes.

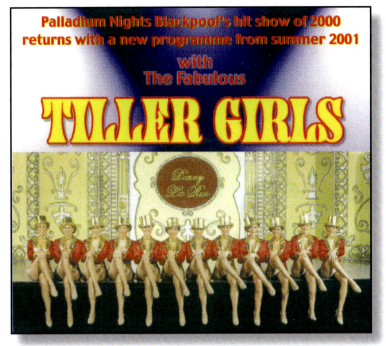

Choreographed by Fay Robinson.

SIXTIES TILLER GIRLS

DATE	SHOW / VENUE / CHARITY	ROYALTY IN ATTENDANCE
DEC. 1988	"JOY TO THE WORLD" ROYAL ALBERT HALL [BBC TV] SAVE THE CHILDREN	PRINCESS ROYAL
APR. 1989	"TERRY THOMAS BENEFIT GALA" THEATRE ROYAL DRURY LANE PARKINSON'S DISEASE SOCIETY	
JUL 1989	"25TH ANNIVERSARY GALA PERFORMANCE CLIFFS PAVILION, WESTCLIFF LOCAL CHARITIES	
DEC 1989	"JOY TO THE WORLD" ROYAL ALBERT HALL [BBC TV] SAVE THE CHILDREN	H.M. QUEEN & PRINCESS ROYAL
MAY 1990	"TAP FOR TELETHON" CROYDON [TELEVISED BY LWT]	
MAY 1990	"ASPECTS OF DANCE" HACKNEY EMPIRE THE SPASTICS SOCIETY	
SEP 1990	"BIRTHDAY CHARITY GALA" BRISTOL HIPPODROME RUSS CONWAY CANCER FUND	
OCT 1990	"LERONA'S CELEBRITY SPECTACULAR LONDON PALLADIUM INT. SPINAL RESEARCH TRUST	THE PRINCESS OF WALES
NOV 1990	"WATER RATS BALL" GROSVENOR HOUSE HOTEL LONDON	PRINCE EDWARD
NOV 1990	"RECORD BREAKERS" [BBC TV] BBC TELEVISION CENTRE CHILDLINE	
DEC 1990	" JOY TO THE WORLD" ROYAL ALBERT HALL [BBC TV]	PRINCESS MARGARET

FEB 1991	"OLD BEN GALA" ROYAL LANCASTER HOTEL NEWS VENDORS BENEVOLENT FUND	
FEB 1991	"SURPRISE SURPRISE" [LWT] LWT STUDIOS LONDON	
MAR 1991	"A GOOD INNINGS" THE HEXAGON, READING THE LORDS TAVERNERS	
APR 1991	"GALA VARIETY PERFORMANCE" ALEXANDRA THEATRE, BIRMINGHAM SAVE THE CHILDREN	PRINCESS ROYAL
MAY 1991	"ASPECTS OF DANCE " HACKNEY EMPIRE SOS. & IMPERIAL CANCER RESEARCH	
JUN 1991	"A ROYAL VARIETY SHOW " THEATRE ROYAL WINDSOR THE BUD FLANAGAN LEUKAEMIA FUND	DUKE OF EDINBURGH
JUN 1991	"HYSTERIA 3 " [CHANNEL 4] LONDON PALLADIUM TERENCE HIGGINS TRUST	
SEP 1991	"BIRTHDAY CHARITY GALA" BRISTOL HIPPODROME RUSS CONWAY CANCER FUND	
OCT 1991	"BERNIE WINTERS' BIG NIGHT OUT" LONDON PALLADIUM RSPCA. & IMPERIAL CANCER RESEARCH	
NOV 1991	"THE ROYAL VARIETY SHOW" VICTORIA PALACE THEATRE EABF.	H.M. THE QUEEN & DUKE OF EDINBURGH
DEC 1991	"A ROYAL GALA SHOW" THEATRE ROYAL WINDSOR WEXHAM PARK CT SCANNER APPEAL	DUCHESS OF YORK

APR 1992	"NIGHT OF NIGHTS" THE BARBICAN HALL LONDON LIGHTHOUSE
MAY 1992	"SUNDAY NIGHT AT THE FLORAL PAVILION" NEW BRIGHTON ST. JOHN'S HOSPICE
MAY 1992	"ASPECTS OF DANCE" HACKNEY EMPIRE IMPERIAL CANCER RESEARCH
JUN 1992	"MR. WONDERFUL" [SAMMY DAVIS JNR] THEATRE ROYAL DRURY LANE IMPERIAL CANCER RESEARCH
JUN 1992	"CELEBRITY CONCERT" SEVENOAKS SCHOOL MINIBUS FOR ROMANIA
SEP 1992	"VOLUNTEER APPEAL" CUMBERLAND HOTEL LONDON BRITISH RED CROSS
OCT 1992	"GENERATION GAME" [BBC TV] BBC TELEVISION CENTRE LONDON
OCT 1992	"THE GREAT EVENT" THE ROYAL FAMILY 40 GLORIOUS YEARS EXCEPT PRINCESS ROYAL THE ROYAL ANNIVERSARY TRUST & H.M. QUEEN MOTHER
MAR 1993	"WAR CHILD" ROYAL FESTIVAL HALL BOSNIA APPEAL
MAR 1993	"SATURDAY ZOO" WITH JONATHON ROSS [CHANNEL 4] [LWT STUDIOS] LONDON
MAY 1993	"ASPECTS OF DANCE" HACKNEY EMPIRE THE PAUL O'GORMAN LEUKAEMIA FUND

OCT 1993	"GALA EVENING" BUXTON OPERA HOUSE IMPERIAL CANCER RESEARCH
OCT 1993	"THE EQUALITY SHOW" LONDON PALLADIUM STONEWALL
NOV 1993	"CHARITY GALA" APOLLO THEATRE OXFORD RUSS CONWAY CANCER FUND & CLIC.
NOV 1993	"WATER RATS BALL" GROSVENOR HOUSE HOTEL LONDON
APR 1994	"LILY SAVAGE SHOW" PALLADIUM THEATRE LONDON
APR 1994	"AEROBOTHON 94" [PUBLICITY] LONDON PALLADIUM VARIOUS CHARITIES
APR 1994	"VIVA CABARET" WITH LILY SAVAGE [CHANNEL 4] LONDON
APR 1994	"VARIETY SPECTACULAR" FLORAL PAVILION NEW BRIGHTON ST. JOHN'S HOSPICE
MAY 1994	"ASPECTS OF DANCE" WIMBLEDON THEATRE PAUL O'GORMAN LEUKAEMIA FUND
JUN 1994	"PAUL MERTON'S HISTORY OF THE PALLADIUM" LONDON [TELEVISED BY THE BBC]
JUN 1994	"GOTTA DANCE" HACKNEY EMPIRE BRITISH RED CROSS & RNIB

MAY 1995	"ASPECTS OF DANCE" WIMBLEDON THEATRE LONDON CHILDREN WITH LEUKAEMIA		
MAY 1995	"LILY SAVAGE SHOW" LIVERPOOL EMPIRE		
JUN 1995	"CABARET" ROYAL LANCASTER HOTEL LONDON CHILDS FINAL WISH		
JUN 1995	"THE BIG BREAKFAST SHOW" (PLANET 24 FOR CHANNEL 4)		
JUL 1995	"LES DAWSON TRIBUTE" GRAND THEATRE BLACKPOOL ARTHRITIS CARE		
JUL 1995	"ROY CASTLE'S CAUSE FOR HOPE" LIVERPOOL EMPIRE		
JUL 1995	"ROY CASTLE'S CAUSE FOR HOPE" LONDON PALLADIUM		
SEP 1995	"A CELEBRATION VARIETY MUSIC HALL" BRISTOL HIPPODROME RUSS CONWAY CANCER FUND		
OCT 1995	"THAT'S ENTERTAINMENT" HACKNEY EMPIRE MARIE CURIE & AGE CONCERN		
OCT 1995	"LILY SAVAGE LIVE AT THE GARRICK" GARRICK THEATRE LONDON (VIDEO)		
OCT 1995	"CELEBRITY GALA EVENING" BUXTON OPERA HOUSE IMPERIAL CANCER RESEARCH FUNDS		
NOV 1995	"A HANDFUL OF KEYS" PRINCE EDWARD THEATRE LONDON CRUSAID & WEST END CARES		
NOV 1995	"CELEBRITY GALA EVENING" WYVERN THEATRE SWINDON NSPCC		
DEC 1995	"GALA" BARN THEATRE OXTED ROY CASTLE'S CAUSE FOR HOPE		
DEC 1995	"JOY TO THE WORLD" ROYAL ALBERT HALL (BBC TV)	THE DUKE AND DUCHESS OF GLOUCESTER	
DEC 1995	"RAGS TO RICHES" SAVOY THEATRE LONDON ACTORS BENEVOLENT FUND & GREEN ROOM CLUB		

SEP 1994	"CHARITY CONCERT" FLORAL PAVILION NEW BRIGHTON APPEAL TO TRAIN McMILLAN NURSES	
OCT 1994	"CELEBRITY GALA EVENING" OPERA HOUSE BUXTON IMPERIAL CANCER RESEARCH	
NOV 1994	"CABARET" CAESARS STREATHAM ROY CASTLE'S CAUSE FOR HOPE	
NOV 1994	"CABARET" DORCHESTER HOTEL LONDON HANDICAPPED CHILDREN	
NOV 1994	"THE MAYORS AUTUMN GALA" HACKNEY EMPIRE BRITISH RED CROSS & RNIB	
DEC 1994	"CARING & SHARING TRUST" COGENHOE NORTHANTS	
FEB 1995	"TELETHON" [SKY TV] VARIETY CLUB	
APR 1995	"LILY SAVAGE SHOW" LIVERPOOL EMPIRE	
APR 1995	"VARIETY SPECTACULAR" FLORAL PAVILION NEW BRIGHTON ST. JOHN'S HOSPICE	
MAY 1995	"VE NIGHT PARTY & CONCERT HYDE PARK CORNER LONDON	H M QUEEN & THE DUKE OF EDINBURGH PRINCESS ROYAL PRINCESS MARGARET DUKE & DUCHESS OF KENT
MAY 1995	"LILY SAVAGE SHOW" LIVERPOOL EMPIRE	
MAY 1995	"CABARET" GROSVENOR HOUSE HOTEL LONDON CHILDREN WITH LEUKAEMIA	

MAR 1996	**LOTTERY INSTANTS TELEVISION COMMERCIAL** **SHEPPERTON STUDIOS**
MAR 1996	**ASPECTS OF DANCE** **DOMINION THEATRE LONDON**
APR 1996	**AUDIENCE WITH LILY SAVAGE TV** **LWT STUDIOS LONDON**
MAY 1996	**WIMBLEDON THEATRE** **PRINCESS ALICE HOSPICE**
MAY 1996	**WEMBLEY ARENA** **DANCEWORLD**
OCT 1996	**BUXTON OPERA HOUSE** **IMPERIAL CANCER RESEARCH**
NOV 1996	**SAVOY THEATRE LONDON** **ARTISTS BENEVOLENT FUND**
DEC 1996	**THE LONDON PALLADIUM** **THE MAGIC SHOW**
OCT 1997	**ROYAL ALBERT HALL** **THE EQUALITY SHOW TO RAISE MONEY** **FOR AIDS CHARITIES**
NOV 1997	**THE LONDON PALLADIUM** **WESTMINSTER ARTS SHOW FOR VARIOUS CHARITIES**
NOV 1997	**THE LONDON PALLADIUM** **THE LADY TAVERNER'S SHOW FOR VARIOUS CHARITIES**
DEC 1997	**HER MAJESTY'S THEATRE LONDON** **MAGIC SHOW FOR THE MAGICIANS CONVENTION**
DEC 1997	**ROYAL ALBERT HALL** **JOY TO THE WORLD FOR SAVE THE CHILDREN**

MAR 1998	BRUCE FORSYTH'S 70TH BIRTHDAY SHOW THE LONDON PALLADIUM [GMTV]
AUG 1998	NEW BRIGHTON FLORAL HALL FOR A LOCAL HOSPICE
SEP 1998	CONGRESS THEATRE EASTBOURNE MAGIC SHOW TWICE NIGHTLY
SEP 1998	WESTMINSTER THEATRE LONDON A VARIETY SHOW TO HELP SAVE THE THEATRE
OCT 1998	LONDON PALLADIUM ALTERNATIVE ARTS SHOW FOR WESTMINSTER COUNCIL
NOV 1998	PALACE THEATRE LONDON A VARIETY SHOW IN AID OF BREAST CANCER
DEC 1998	HER MAJESTY'S THEATRE LONDON MAGIC SHOW
MAR 1999	HACKNEY EMPIRE A VARIETY SHOW TO SUPPORT WOMEN'S DAY
MAY 1999	EASTWOOD STUDIO THEATRE 'KONCERT FOR KOSOVO' TO HELP RAISE FUNDS FOR REFUGEES
JUNE 1999	COTTON'S FARMHOUSE IN NORTHAMPTON CARING & SHARING SHOW FOR THOSE WHO ATTEND THE FARM
SEP 1999	KING GEORGES HALL BLACKBURN A VARIETY SHOW TO HELP SAVE THE THEATRE
OCT 1999	LLANDUDNO'S NORTH WALES THEATRE SHOW FOR THE MAGIC CONVENTION
DEC 1999	HER MAJESTY'S THEATRE LONDON MAGIC SHOW FOR THE MAGICIAN'S CONVENTION

MAR 2000	LONDON PALLADIUM ALTERNATIVE ARTS SHOW FOR THE ALTERNATIVE ARTS CHARITIES
MAR 2000	SUNDAY NIGHT AT THE LONDON PALLADIUM
JULY 2000	G MEX CENTRE MANCHESTER A TAPATHON WITH WAYNE SLEEP DANCE FOR CHILDREN'S CHARITIES
JULY 2000	COTTON'S FARMHOUSE IN NORTHAMPTON CARING AND SHARING SHOW FOR THOSE WHO ATTEND THE FARM
SEP 2000	CONGRESS THEATRE EASTBOURNE RUSS CONWAYS'S 75TH BIRTHDAY CELEBRATIONS
SEP 2000	LONDON PALLADIUM FOR THE ROYAL MASONIC VARIETY SHOW
SEP 2000	CONGRESS THEATRE EASTBOURNE MAGIC SHOW FOR THE MAGICIAN'S CONVENTION
OCT 2000	THEATRE ROYAL BUXTON A VARIETY SHOW IN AID OF CANCER RESEARCH
NOV 2000	KILROY TV SHOW ELSTREE STUDIOS
DEC 2000	HER MAJESTY'S THEATRE LONDON MAGIC SHOW FOR THE MAGICIAN'S CONVENTION

MAR 2001	THE KENNETH MORE THEATRE ILFORD DANCEWORLD
MAY 2001	MARLOW THEATRE CANTERBURY DAVE LEE CHARITY NIGHT
MAY 2001	THE ROYAL ALBERT HALL DUKE OF EDINBURGH'S 80TH BIRTHDAY SHOW
JUNE 2001	THE WESTMINSTER THEATRE LONDON TRIBUTE TO RUSS CONWAY
AUG 2001	THE KENNETH MORE THEATRE ILFORD CHARITY SHOW FOR JEWISH SERVICEMEN
SEP 2001	CONNISTON HALL BRISTOL CANCER HOSPICE FOR THE LATE RUSS CONWAY
SEP 2001	ROYAL HOSPITAL CHELSEA MAJOR MICHAEL PARKER'S ARMY RE-UNION
DEC 2001	THE HAYMARKET THEATRE LONDON THE MAGIC SHOW
MAR 2002	THE KENNETH MORE THEATRE ILFORD CHARITY PERFORMANCE
APR 2002	CHUMS CHARITY PERFORMANCE IN A HOTEL ON THE ISLE OF DOGS LONDON
APR 2002	MARLOW THEATRE CANTERBURY DAVE LEE CHARITY NIGHT
JUNE 2002	HER MAJESTY THE QUEEN'S GOLDEN JUBILEE BUCKINGHAM PALACE
JULY 2002	LOWRY CENTRE MANCHESTER CHARITY FOR HOME FOR AGED ACTORS
SEP 2002	FASHION SHOW LIVERPOOL PRINCE OF WALES TRUST

	THIS MORNING TV SHOW TIGHTS AND FASHION	
MAY 2003	MARLOW THEATRE CANTERBURY DAVE LEE CHARITY NIGHT	
OCT 2003	LADY RATLINGS BALL	
NOV 2003	STOCKPORT THEATRE ALZHEIMER'S CHARITY WITH THE CAST OF CORONATION STREET	
JAN 2004	GREENWICH THEATRE MAX WALL SOCIETY	
MAR 2004	MANCHESTER OLD TRAFFORD LADIES CHARITY SHOW	
APR 2004	OPERA HOUSE MANCHESTER VARIETY CLUB WITH THE CORONATION STREET CAST AND PAUL O'GRADY	
MAY 2004	MARLOW THEATRE CANTERBURY DAVE LEE CHILDREN OF KENT	
MAY 2004	THIS MORNING TV LONDON	
MAY 2004	GRAND THEATRE LEEDS BREAST CANCER WITH CORONATION STREET CAST	
JUNE 2004	HER MAJESTY'S THEATRE LONDON HANDS ON EVENT CHARITY	
JULY 2004	BUCKINGHAM PALACE GARDEN PARTY NOT FORGOTTEN ASSOCIATION	PRINCESS ANNE
JULY 2004	THEATRE ROYAL WINDSOR BUD FLANAGAN CHARITY	DUKE OF EDINBURGH
NOV 2004	PAUL O'GRADY SHOW LWT LONDON	
DEC 2004	ST. JAMES PALACE NOT FORGOTTEN ASSOCIATION	PRINCE CHARLES

JAN 2005	BONNINGTON HOTEL LONDON LADY RATLINGS
FEB 2005	ASHCROFT HALLS CROYDON CHARITY SHOW
MAR 2005	ILFORD DANCE SHOW
MAR 2005	ILFORD LADY RATLINGS
MAY 2005	MARLOW THEATRE CANTERBURY DAVE LEE CHARITY SHOW
JULY 2005	CONCERT ARTISTES ASSOCIATION LONDON
OCT 2005	GROSVENOR HOUSE HOTEL LONDON LADY RATLINGS BALL
MAR 2006	KENNETH MORE THEATRE ILFORD DANCE SHOW
APR 2006	MARLOWE THEATRE CANTERBURY DAVE LEE CHARITY SHOW
APR 2006	PARADISE ROOM BLACKPOOL CABARET FOR MARK RAFFLES
MAR 2007	YORK HOUSE RICHMOND CHARITY EVENING
MAR 2007	KENNETH MORE THEATRE ILFORD DANCE SHOW
APR 2007	MARLOWE THEATRE CANTERBURY DAVE LEE CHARITY SHOW
JUNE 2007	GREENWICH NAVAL COLLEGE NOT FORGOTTEN ASSOCIATION

JULY 2007	BUCKINGHAM PALACE GARDEN PARTY NOT FORGOTTEN ASSOCIATION	
SEP 2007	GALANOS HOUSE SOUTHAM FETE OPENING NOT FORGOTTEN ASSOCIATION	
OCT 2007	HAMMERSMITH TOWN HALL HELP THE AGED	
OCT 2007	GROSVENOR HOUSE HOTEL LONDON LADY RATLINGS BALL	
MAR 2008	KENNETH MORE THEATRE ILFORD DANCE SHOW	
MAY 2008	PAUL O'GRADY SHOW TV SHOW LWT LONDON	
SEP 2008	LONDON PALLADIUM "FLY WITH THE STARS" FOR THE BATTLE OF BRITAIN MEMORIAL TRUST	PRINCE MICHAEL OF KENT
OCT 2008	HEATHROW AIRPORT DUTY FREE PROMOTION	

In 1984 I purchased a brand new one-bedroomed house in Wallasey in a beautiful spot overlooking the River Mersey. I then had two mortgages, my little house and half of mum's, and I had the investment bug. I'd learnt the hard way by working and making my money work for me. I put money into stocks and shares bonds ISAs and had already started plans for my private pension, for which I got tax relief. I soon realised that if I wanted nice things and some luxuries in life, I had to work hard to make them happen. As a child, we always seemed to be living on the breadline. I knew from my childhood that things never came easy and weren't just handed to you on a plate. I never had holidays as a child, but I appreciated the money my parents spent on my dancing. I knew they couldn't afford both. I believe what you've never had, you never miss. As long as I had my dancing I was happy.

While doing a summer season in Blackpool one year, I booked and paid for mum to bring my two brothers, Tim and Jeremy, for a few days' break. I was lucky because I was now working in seaside places so I felt life was one big holiday, and work was the most wonderful hobby which I got paid for and was a dream come true!

Two or three years into my 12 year stay at the health club, I was promoted to managing director. I was really happy working there. I didn't care how many hours I put in. I could and would stay all day and night, so much so that some of the gym members thought I was a partner in the business. I was dedicated, memberships were doing really well, and around 1990 we opened another club. In Wallasey I organised a big charity event at the health club with instructors and gym members. We did twenty-four hour non-stop aerobics which raised over £3,000 for Save the Children. This event was supported by Radio Merseyside. I was interviewed by Billy Butler who praised all involved for their wonderful contributions and effort. It was quite exhausting for all instructors involved who kept the uninterrupted connection throughout when taking over from another instructor who was having a quick glass of water and a banana to refuel.

In 1986 mum's health was giving me concern. She had a number of blackouts and on one occasion fell and broke her arm. She had been on medication for rheumatoid arthritis, and the year previously she had her wrist in a splint. In 1987 she developed a thrombosis in her leg and spent a few days in hospital. On the phone when I spoke to her, she said she had been having very bad headaches and her vision hadn't been good, and she was violently sick. I knew by her voice she wasn't her usual self. When she told me she had lost interest in doing her crosswords, I knew something was very wrong.

On one of my weekend visits home to see mum, I called her GP to come and see her. Arrangements were made for mum to go into hospital for some tests. They didn't come up with anything positive other than her bad arthritis and circulation, and she had by now developed Type 2 diabetes for which medication was given. Just before Christmas in 1988 after another one of her dizzy spells, mum had another fall and was back in hospital where she stayed until I picked her up when I went home for my Christmas break.

I remember it very clearly. I went straight to the hospital to collect her. She couldn't walk very well and seemed very unsteady on her feet. It was quite a walk back to the car so I asked for a wheelchair. I got her into the car then drove home. I got mum into the house and sat her down. It was very cold, I put a blanket round her and set too to light the fire. I raked the ashes out, chopped the sticks, laid the paper, sticks and coal, and put a light to it. I put the shovel in front of the fire with a big sheet of newspaper across to draw it quicker. I had to keep an eye on it otherwise the paper would catch fire, blow up the chimney and set fire to the chimney. While the fire was taking hold, I went into the kitchen to put the kettle on to make mum a cup of tea. Mum called out to me "Fay, come here". I dashed straight into the living room thinking something had happened to the fire. Mum said again "come here, love". She put her arms around me and said thank you for bringing me home. I could feel tears in my eyes. I didn't want mum to see me crying so I immediately went back into the kitchen to make the tea. After our evening meal, we both sat in front of a nice cosy fire and watched television.

The news that night was of the Lockerbie Air Disaster. It was a Wednesday. Mum was very upset about it. It was to be the very last thing she saw on television, and the very last conversation we had together. The following morning I found mum in a coma in a state of deep unconsciousness. I was in a state of shock not knowing what to do. My first reaction was to phone her GP. I suppose I should have phoned for an ambulance, but what was going through my mind was that she had only come out of hospital the night before, and I knew she was very ill and wanted to be in her beloved home.

When Dr Khan, her GP, arrived he said she was very sick with bronchopneumonia and had had a cerebral thrombosis of the right side and interstitial pulmonary fibrosis. He said he could get her into hospital, but it was very unlikely she would pull through. All they would be able to do was make her comfortable or she could be looked after at home. I asked if this was life threatening and he said "I'm afraid so, and you know your mum was only waiting for you to come home". This brought a flood of tears rolling down my face; a quick decision had to be made, and I chose to look after her at home. This is something I will always have to live with, wondering if I had made the right decision. If she was going to leave me, I wanted to be with her. I cared for her, washed her, changed her and spent days talking to her even though there was no reply.

Mum once said to me that when someone is in a deep coma, always be careful what you or someone says in front of them as their hearing is the last to leave them. With this in mind, I talked to her. I held her hand and sometimes she felt agitated. I said "I'm here mum, I'm not going back, I'm going to stay with you. I'm not going to leave you." I felt her squeeze my hand, and I know she understood and heard what I'd said. This made me feel that this was what she wanted. I had a visit from one of the nurses who said I was doing a good job, and that they couldn't have looked after her any better. Christmas Day came and my oldest sister brought my Christmas dinner round. I sat next to mum with my dinner on my lap. There was just the two of us. The rest of my family had small children so it was right they should be together on Christmas Day. My Christmas break from work was coming to an end but I couldn't leave mum. I phoned Mr Birchall at the health club. I explained how ill mum was and he said take as long as you need. Which is what I did.

On 31 December (New Year's Eve) at 11:10 am mum passed away peacefully. I was with her to the end. She was only 67 years old. I now felt totally on my own; with the rest of my family settled, I had to rethink where I was going. I seemed to be asking myself a lot of questions: "What will I do? What do I want? Will I be able to carry on doing what I enjoy work-wise?". The answer to this was probably not, as working in the gym was becoming physically demanding on my joints. Having worked physically all my life from being a little girl, and with at least ten years left before my pension, I thought if I don't change tracks, I'll never see my pension!

I had a problem with my knee on which I had had a small operation. This was mainly so I could continue my workload, and my back problem which I'd had for many years. In fact, on one occasion while working in Birmingham, I had a flare-up and was sent for an x-ray. While in front of two specialists discussing my problem, I was told I had spina bifida at the base of my spine. This was something I was obviously born with, and as it hadn't given me severe problems before, it was very unlikely to. The only thing I could never do was to sit cross-legged on the floor because two vertebrae were fused together which makes the base of my spine very solid.

Hearing this news, I thought how lucky I'd been to be able to dance with my adorable Tiller Girls.

As I got older I had to learn to live with this problem I had with my back and adapt myself accordingly. Sometimes the pain and discomfort was so severe I couldn't get out of bed. My back felt locked, set solid with no movement at all, and it was quite frightening. I'd roll out of bed like a huge lump and hang on to the window sill in case my legs collapsed underneath me. I would shout out with the pain as I tried to get to the bathroom. I spent many years having these flare-ups but I learnt to cope. I knew it was very severe if I couldn't put my socks and underwear on. I've worked through many shows with much discomfort. The saying in show business is "the show must go on". I even struggled to work while having physio and traction at the local hospital. If I could get out of bed and get dressed, nothing would stop me dancing or getting on with my life.

Through experience I've found that physical activity can slash the risk of disability and ease the pain of a range of conditions, including arthritis, back pain and brittle bone disease. Exercise is one of the best things you can do if you have arthritis or a musculoskeletal complaint. One should keep moving as much as one can and exercise to the best of one's ability. Listen to your body like me: if you have a flare-up, when the pain is acute, take a rest, but never take to your bed for days on end as this won't help you gain your movement back.

The human body is designed to move and inactivity is harmful to tissues in and around the joints. So to prolong the life and movements of your joints, you should remain active. Taking too many drugs can upset the stomach, and eating certain foods can play a big part in some flare-ups of the joints. I'm not saying you should be jogging or jumping around; just don't be afraid to exercise. I would recommend swimming, walking, cycling, fitness classes, callanetics, pilates, to include stretching exercises, which all strengthen the muscles and core of the body and improve your posture and flexibility and keep your body moving.

Over the years I've been very surprised when people compliment me on my posture and how straight I am. If only they knew what pain and discomfort I've gone through; sometimes the pain was excruciating and the slightest move sent my muscles into spasm. My body then became lopsided and very stiff, with one hip higher than the other, and I knew then that I had to refer to my bed to try and straighten myself up. I was absolutely gutted when this occurred at a time when I wanted to give a special performance, be it for charity or otherwise. I once had a full diary of beauty appointments, and it put lots of stress on me to deliver these treatments. I never wanted to let anyone down.

Scene Thirteen

Moving On A Different Route

In the early 1990s the health club I was working for held interviews for new instructors which were to staff the opening of a new health club, and with the help of myself, we chose three or four with excellent qualifications. With the success of the Wallasey health club and the experience, Mr Birchall, myself and the team knew what we were looking for.

When it came to training these instructors to our standards and to the way we wanted the club to run, one of them was impertinent, in fact, very disrespectful, even rude at times! She wouldn't accept any skills or techniques of our way of doing things, and did her very best to ignore me. She was always ill or not feeling well to avoid any training sessions, and although her CV was very good and impressive, I was beginning to wonder if she had bluffed her way in. From my experience, what looked good on paper, if it couldn't be put into practice, didn't make her or any other instructor a good teacher.

I would prefer it the other way round: someone who has lots of enthusiasm, is keen on safety, polite, helpful, caring, has a nice personality and above all is able to work as part of a team, willing to learn and improve anything for the benefit of the members and the health club. In this case, her attitude in front of the other instructors was giving me concern. I was hoping it wouldn't rub off on them.

While the staff at the new club were left to run it, I was back in Wallasey when I became suspicious and dubious. I suspected something was going on, and was distrustful when the management decided to take a popular class out of our class programme. I knew this was a bad mistake and the Wallasey members wouldn't like it. I didn't know of anyone who would want to take something off the shelf if it was selling well! This particular class was very popular and always carried good class numbers. I was very hurt by this, even more so as it was never discussed with me. There may have been a very good reason for it, but for me it would have to be good to take it from our timetable. My suspicion was with this particular instructor. I felt I was being bullied as it appeared to have been her idea and she said it wasn't safe. I think it was because she didn't want to take the class herself.

At the time I was just getting over losing mum. I was going through the menopause and my hormones were playing me up. There were changes going on inside my mind and body which appeared to be sending anxiety signals, and my brain chemistry was playing games. I wished I'd been left alone in Wallasey.

At the new health club they could have made changes as and when they needed. I was so upset, I chose to leave. It was my decision and no-one else's, but I must say, it felt like a bereavement. I had many, many happy years there.

After putting this behind me, I took myself on to a different route. I was now back at school and training to be a beauty therapist at the Lillian Maund Beauty School in Chester, and a new career had materialised. I proved to myself that even in your fifties, you are never too old to change direction and learn a new skill. My knowledge of anatomy and physiology, which I had gained from my years in the fitness industry, helped me tremendously, and with hard work I became a qualified beauty therapist.

I opened my first beauty room within 'Physical' a health club a short distance away from where I lived. I worked part-time to get myself established and to gain experience. I then saw an advertisement for a beauty room to rent working within 'FITNESS FIRST' health club in Bromborough. This was a huge company which had a chain of health clubs all over the country. I arranged to have an interview for which I needed a couple of references. I rang Mr Birchall for a reference, which he very kindly did for me, and I received it the following morning. He also added a little note in it to say he regretted how we had parted company, and that it must have been a misunderstanding on both parts. He asked would I like to have dinner with him and his wife, Lynn. I was very tempted to accept his invitation, but I had by then put lots of hard work and money into training for a new career, so I had to continue moving on.

I accepted the beauty room at Fitness First which over the weeks turned out to be very expensive. It was like having a second mortgage for a huge mansion! The room was tiny, and after approaching the management over the monthly rent, it was decided I could have a reduction if I did a fitness class free of charge for them. This I did for a few more weeks, but the only people benefiting was Fitness First. I could see my bank balance dwindling even further. I needed to move as soon as possible.

It was around this time that I "put two and two together" and worked out that beauty doesn't go well in a fitness club. I'd learnt the hard way that people join a fitness club to get fit, and when paying a monthly membership they liked to use their time working out not to have an extra expense to pay for a treatment. It all sounds very exciting when you are told how many members walk through the door, and you think maybe you'll have it made in a big way. I put it down to experience.

Then, how lucky was I to see a position for a beauty therapist within an exclusive hairdressing salon, Robbi Ross Hair and Beauty. I didn't delay sending my CV; I hand delivered it! This also gave me the opportunity to see the salon. It was perfect: in a nice position, beautiful and clean and nicely decorated, and I could see myself working there. Things went well at my interview with Mr Ross, and a date was set for my opening. The staff were very polite and looked very professional in their white uniforms. They also made me very welcome.

In between my appointments, treatments and bookings, I spent two hours each day posting flyers through letter boxes of streets I had mapped out as I walked down them. After a few weeks my clientele was picking up nicely and my product stock needed topping up. It was at this stage that Mr Robbi Ross said, as he knew nothing about beauty, would I like to take the beauty salon over and rent my room upstairs. I saw this as a nice opportunity and accepted his offer. As the months went by, my business was doing well, my clientele was showing regular monthly appointments, and I was working to my capacity and physical mental ability. There were some treatments that put a lot of stress on my back; for example, full body massage or leg waxing. It was a very nice feeling to be successful. It was at this stage that I could have taken on another beautician, but I was happy working on my own without the worry of anyone letting me down or not turning up, and no insurance stamps or holiday pay to give you a headache. So I chose to stay working for myself and close the salon when I needed a break or holiday.

By now, most, if not all of my clientele, were regular monthly customers, and after ten years I had got to know them quite well, in fact, one or two have become my friends. Over the years I had some very nice clients of mixed age groups. One of them, an elderly lady 93 years of age, took great pride in how she looked. I used to do her a manicure and the occasional face wax. During conversation or while I was painting her nails, she would fall asleep and I found that I was talking to myself. She was a very independent lady, too. She wouldn't let you help her down the stairs and would say "I have stairs at home you know and manage quite well, and if you don't use your legs you lose them". How right she was. She would have her hair done by Robbi, and I often caught her having a cat-nap under the hairdryer.

I was once put in an embarrassing situation. One of my clients was a petite, blind, very clever young lady who was a lot older than what she looked. She was born without any eyeball sockets, and had only a row of lovely long eyelashes. Her eyebrows were quite thick and almost reached her eyelashes. I would shape her eyebrows so that she had a nice gap in between. On one of her appointments, her mum asked me to do her a manicure; I think it was for her birthday. When it came to putting the nail polish on her nails, I thought how do I ask her what colour polish would she like? Anyway, I did and with much confidence she came straight out with "Oh, I'll have blue because I support Everton". It was hard to imagine how she would never have known what the colour blue looked like, but how she associated blue with her football team, of which she was a great supporter. One can only admire and respect one with these kind of disabilities, and appreciate most things in life that we take for granted. She was such an inspiration and always so cheerful.

My years in my beauty salon were happy years, and I also had the pleasure of still being asked to perform in our charity shows with the 60s Tiller Girls. This always lifted my spirit and enthusiasm. It gave me a purpose for life. It was working for myself that now made all this possible, and I had the best of both worlds.

At the beginning of the year 2000, the question kept being asked "How long are we as senior ladies going to be able to carry on kicking our legs up"! It was decided that while we still looked good and could perform our routines well, and still get into our costumes, we would carry on. We left it to Miss Wendy Clarke to tell us when to hang up our dancing shoes. We wanted people to say we were good, not "aren't they good for their age".

As the years went by, the line-up was getting shorter and shorter as the girls dropped out one by one. It was usually family illnesses or the Big C. This serious illness took some of our beloved Tiller Girls' lives. Occasionally it was because we had seen ourselves on TV and didn't like the way we looked. This was the professionalism in us. It always had to be right and feel right.

We had on a number of occasions at a charity show decided it was going to be our last performance, but then another show came along, then another and another. It was beginning to feel that some of us couldn't let go, but it was such an honour to be asked. For me it was the Paul O'Grady afternoon show that was to be my last performance. We were asked to do part of a Tiller Girl routine, not a full routine, so it was quite short. At rehearsals, for the first time in my life, I couldn't get my breath. I had no strength in my legs, and could barely get up off my knee at the end of the routine. This was the most frightening thing. I could hardly walk up the stairs. I didn't say anything to anyone as I held on to the handrail walking up the stairs. I knew something was seriously wrong, and immediately thought I was pretty close to having a heart attack. At that very moment I decided that was my last show.

Being in the fitness industry, I'd made a habit of checking my blood pressure regularly. As soon as I got home that was the first thing I did. I couldn't get a reading; it was showing up as error on my monitor. A visit to the doctor put me straight. After an ECG in her surgery, my GP said I had a problem with my heart. I could not believe it. I'd worked hard at keeping myself fit and healthy or so I thought. It was treatable with medication, and an appointment was made for me to see a heart specialist. I said to my GP that I was on my way for a swim and she said "I don't think so". I always kept up my exercise routine, and every week I would walk, ride my bike and swim. It made me feel good about myself, and I was hoping it would prolong my life, along with my healthy eating plan.

A few weeks later after seeing a heart specialist, and after numerous tests, including another ECG and an echocardiogram, I was diagnosed with atrial fibrillation and a slight leakage through the mitral valve. Having an under-active thyroid didn't help. Atrial fibrillation is quite a common thing, but with medication and regular check-ups I keep on top of everything and get on with my life. After having a chest x-ray the radiologist told me for my age I had a very tiny heart. I looked at this as a good thing because as you age your heart usually enlarges! So I guess I'm lucky.

Scene Fourteen

1960s PALLADIUM TILLERS
MY TRIP TO NEW YORK

In November 1999 five of the Tiller Girls, including myself, went on a short trip to New York: Kath, June, Rosalie, Hazel and me, and a boy dancer, Rodney, a friend of Rosalie made our group up to six. We had heard so much about Radio City Music Hall and the Rockettes, a dance troupe that followed our footsteps and style of dance. We wanted to see them and even try and meet up with them if we could.

We saved our pennies and off we went – NEW YORK HERE WE COME! The northern girls, Hazel, Kath and myself, flew from Manchester, Rosalie, June and Rodney flew from London Heathrow. We had arranged to meet up with them at J F Kennedy Airport, NEW YORK.

Our flight arrived first. We had a couple of hours to wait during which time we saw an office advertising stretched limo cars. We thought "let's do it in style". We worked out how much it would cost, splitting the expense between six of us, so we went for it and booked one. I decided to find some white paper and write TILLER GIRLS on it, and as the London girls had Rodney with them, another sheet that said TILLER BOY. We had seen this done on as number of occasions when celebrities are met by a chauffeur on arrival at the station or airports.

As the Heathrow flight came in we went to the arrival gate and held up our white sheets of paper. When they saw us they had such a laugh and were so surprised when we told them there was a LIMO waiting for us. They thought it was a joke. We had fun in the limo driving into New York City in style.

On arrival in New York after booking into our hotel, we met up in the lounge and planned our stay. To get everything in we had a tight schedule. We had to book our tickets for the shows we wanted to see. First stop – guess where? Radio City Music Hall – I was so excited. When we had booked our tickets, we made a few enquiries about going to see the "Rockettes". We were "over the moon" when we were told we could book a backstage tour and meet up later with one of the Rockettes, which is what we did. We were like little children going to the theatre for the first time. The show was amazing, absolutely fabulous when the Rockettes spread across the stage in a line-up of 36. I thought GOSH, I wished I was one of them. The show was magical and for me like a dream come true. We couldn't stop talking about it.

It's hard to believe that our mentor, John Tiller, started all this unique kind of dancing "Precision" way back in 1886. When a troupe of Tiller Girls were working in America they took America by storm. The Tiller Girls must have played a huge part in this style of dancing, and left an opportunity for Russell Markerts to take to the stage on 17 October 1925 16 "MISSOURI ROCKETS". The Radio City opening night took two years to plan, and opened on 27 December 1932 when the 36 precision dancers were called "THE ROXYETTES". In 1934 their name changed to RADIO CITY ROCKETTES. Russell Markerts was the Rockettes' director and choreographer until 1971, the exact year my contract was cancelled for the Palladium TV Series.

On our tour backstage at Radio City it was an honour to be recognised by a photo of the TIRELESS TILLERS arriving in New York in 1886. These photographs were in the corridor at Radio City. How proud I felt that our John Tiller started his unique style of dancing more than 35 years before the famous Rockettes, and I was pleased to see a photo of the Tillers in place in this famous theatre Radio City. After our tour backstage we were taken to a room where we had a chance to speak to one of the Rockettes dancers. It was a privilege for us to be able to ask a few questions. I asked about the height of the girls in line. The Tiller Girls always had the shorter girls in the centre, but the Rockettes had the shorter girls on each end of the line. That seemed strange to me because most of the taller girls had longer legs, except me, and due to the formations required in the routines, nearly always had further to travel. Dancing ability was the same: a good all round dancer (meaning skilled at tap, modern, jazz and ballet). What a night at Radio City. I couldn't sleep that night. To this day I wish I could have been part of that line of dancers.

Back stage tour of Radio City New York. Tireless Tillers arriving in 1986.

The following morning we got a taxi to the ferry for our trip to The Statue of Liberty on an island in New York Harbour. Not many people know, but this Statue has a very interesting history. I found it most intriguing, and thought that if history was as good as this when I was at school, I would have done much better with my education. I may have come first instead of bottom in my history exams. My brochure gave some wonderful history information.

A young French sculptor named Frederic Auguste Barthold visited America in 1871. When he saw Bedloes Island in New York Harbour he knew it was the right place for a statue he wanted to build. This statue was to be very special and was to be a present from the people of France to the people of America as a remembrance of the old friendship between the two countries. The statue would be a woman called "Liberty", and she would hold a lamp in her raised hand to welcome people who came to America.

The statue would be large as Barthold wanted people to be able to climb up inside of it and look out over the harbour from the crown and torch, and this is what he did. There is a lift to take you part way up, or you could take the stairs all the way! Being Tiller Girls and super fit, so we thought, off we all went. We didn't think we would have the energy to climb to the crown, 168 steps, and the higher we went the narrower the staircase became. I felt we were just going round in circles. We were determined to make it to the top; I was anyway. Poor June was afraid of heights, but being a true Tiller plodded on in fear. We eventually made it to the top of the crown. Looking through the small windows over the harbour was spectacular.

As all the ships pass her, she has welcomed millions of people arriving in New York. In her raised right hand she holds a beacon of light to welcome voyagers to America. In the crown there are seven spikes which represent the seven seas and seven continents of the world. In her left arm she holds a tablet inscribed in Roman numerals with the date 4 July 1776 – the date of the signing of the Declaration of Independence, and every year on the Fourth of July the United States of America celebrates its independence.

It was a French engineer who constructed the skeleton of the Statue (as well as the Eiffel Tower); his name was Alexandre Gustave Eiffel. So, much to my surprise, the French played a huge part in all of this. What a coincidence, too, I was more surprised to find out that the Statue was completed in *1886*, the year our John Tiller Girls opened in America.

After a tiring morning walking up and down steps and learning all the history of Radio City and the Statue of Liberty, it was a quick dash for the ferry, into a taxi and on to the theatre for an afternoon performance of 'Annie Get Your Gun' with Bernadette Peters. This Irving Berlin Musical had some great music and a well known story, but for me it lacked the glamour, colour and feathers.

Then, after Radio City, anything for me would be dull, or maybe it was because I was hungry, not having the time to eat properly. We enjoyed a meal at "Sardis" a restaurant for people in show business. Can't think who we were expecting to meet in there – maybe Frank Sinatra – but being in the theatre profession we had to pay it a visit. The walls were decorated with all the famous stars' autographed photos. I thought, I have a selection of the same at home, but mine are all in a box.

A visit to the theatre to see "Chicago" was our next port of call. I loved the dancing in this musical. I'm a great fan of Bob Fosse and his style; I loved it. In fact, I used his style of dance when

I choreographed the Danny La Rue Show. The tickets were 65 dollars which twelve years ago was a lot of money.

Skating in the square, a trip to Central Park, is where I remember Maurice Chevalier filmed "Gi Gi" with Audrey Hepburn. A day shopping followed before our flight home. The buzz for me was still Radio City Music Hall, and I can't wait to see it again. The memories and history left me flabbergasted. Going to New York gave me lots of confidence, ideas and motivation. I wished I'd conquered New York earlier.

Tiller sisters together in New York.
The excitement of it all. Radio City Music Hall.

Scene Fifteen

Winning Line

In September 1999 while doing a show in Llandudno for the Magic Convention with the 60s Tiller Girls, it came up in conversation that Danny La Rue was going to Blackpool for a summer season in the year 2000. To celebrate this millennium year, he was going to star in the show at the Blackpool Winter Gardens Theatre, and it was going to be called "Palladium Nights". I'd read about this in The Stage paper. It was also going to involve the re-opening of this theatre as a few years ago this music hall type venue had been part-dismantled. It had been taken apart piece by piece: all the seating, stage and dressing rooms had been taken out, and it was left with just a shell.

As the show was going to be called "Palladium Nights", it seemed pretty obvious they would be using a line of Tiller Girls. I'd read that Mr Duggie Chapman, a well-known northern showman, was going to produce the show with the Tiller Girls, and that he had had permission from Mr Robert Luff to do so. I thought how wonderful that someone was brave enough to bring variety back after such a long spell due to the drawn out recession.

Wondering who was going to do the choreography for the Tiller Girls, a dream and ambition of mine, I wrote to Mr Chapman with my CV and asked if he would be requiring any help in this direction. Days went by while I waited anxiously for Mr Chapman's reply - a letter, a phone call, and then one morning the phone rang and it was him. "Miss Robinson" he said "I think we should meet".

After this telephone conversation, which led to an interview where we exchanged ideas and plans, he asked if I would choreograph the show.

I felt this was a turning point in my career and a lifelong ambition of mine. I was under the impression at first that it would be for the speciality routines of the Tiller Girls, being the distinguished precision work that the Tiller Girls were known for, but it was for the whole production and involved other members of the cast, including Mr Danny La Rue. I was ecstatic, thrilled and overjoyed with excitement that I was given this opportunity. It was splendid to be involved with the costume designs, too, of which I played a big part.

I knew because of the time schedule this was going to involve a lot of hard work, both for me and a new line of girls who would be professional dancers with experience but who would have never worked a Tiller line. It was most unusual to have a completely all new line of girls; it was very rare and unfamiliar not to have some original Tiller Girls in a line-up to help support, say, three or four new girls that were brought into a line. This was always a normal thing to do by the Tiller Schools, but all the original Tiller Girls had gone due to the recession and the John Tiller Schools had closed their doors.

As rehearsal time was going to be short due to a very tight budget, it was now down to me to choreograph the routines which I set out on paper without the girls. I represented each girl with a cross, and moved the crosses accordingly. So, when rehearsals started, I had the routines set in my mind for the twelve dancers, and planned they would have to learn a routine a day to stay on track.

Being overwhelmed with excitement that I had conquered my dream, I felt a huge responsibility. I had a name to live up to; our mentor, John Tiller, had very high standards. I wanted him, if he were there, to feel proud that I was taking his name forward to the next generation; his girls had been performing for over one hundred and twenty years!

The pressure and responsibility on me was enormous. There were questions I was asking myself. I wouldn't know the girls; would they take the discipline; would they work as a team not as an individual; would they be enthusiastic, keen and eager for perfection for the flawlessness in our routines? These were all the things I was feeling. As it was going to be up to me to make the right choice at the audition, it would be a gamble not knowing the girls.

I was still working in my beauty salon and on the new line-up we had to audition for. After a few weeks when everything was planned and all in order regarding music, costumes and choreography, a date was set for me to audition for the brand new line of Tiller Girls at the Blackpool Winter Gardens. Apart from the 60s Tillers performing our one-off shows for charity, it was some years since a line of Tiller Girls had been booked for a season show, and this one was to run for seventeen weeks. For me it was a privilege and a great honour to have been given this moment and chance.

On the day of the audition, everything went according to plan. The turn out was excellent, and there were over two hundred dancers. As the girls were arriving, I had butterflies in my stomach. I began to feel how I felt when I auditioned for the Tiller Girls some forty-five years ago. I remember thinking "will I be good enough, will I be slim enough?". The biggest blow or failure was being able to do the work but your height letting you down because you didn't slot into the line. I knew as the girls were arriving that some were going to be lucky, but because of the turn out, a lot were going to be disappointed.

It was tough choosing a line of girls with good enduring energy and strength. Only a Tiller Girl would know how hard one had to work and with what stamina was required. Then there was the line-up height-wise to consider, checking that their shoulders and heads all blended in to make a perfect line. Tall girls seemed hard to find. After a long day, I finally chose the twelve lucky ladies. It was an exciting day for everyone with lots of press in attendance, along with the TV news and cameras.

With the audition over, it was time for the girls' measurements and shoe sizes to be taken. They would have their first fitting during their week of rehearsals, which was slotted in when they met up with the rest of the company, and the hard work was to begin.

Audition and choreographed by me. The new Tiller Girls.

At this point, I would like to remind members of the public and a few friends that the show was put together in less than a week. The girls had five days to learn five production numbers, three of which were Tiller speciality routines. Bear in mind, not one of the dancers were experienced Tillers and they had never worked together before. As original Tiller Girls know, they always had a week's school rehearsal to learn a routine, even if most of them were longstanding Tiller Girls with possibly a few years' experience, or there may have been two or three new girls introduced into their line, they were there to support them.

With most of the feedback we had, this new line of girls did an extraordinary and remarkable job in the time allocated, and I thought they were excellent. Then I would say that, they were my "WINNING LINE".

The Winter Gardens Theatre had been part-demolished. The stage was reconstructed, it was remodelled, renovated and restored with huge panels; there were plenty of joins in it and it was solid. This brings me to the spring and bounce you would normally find in a proper stage. This temporary stage had none of that which made it hard going underfoot. The dressing rooms backstage were handy, convenient, transportable cabins. Mr Danny La Rue had a huge area set up like a green room in a theatre as a so-called rest area. There was always champagne on tap and drinks for his visiting guests which he always made welcome, and he had lots of charm and hospitality, warmth and kindness when greeting any guest after the shows in the evenings.

Me with Danny La Rue.

We had lots to learn and do during our weekly rehearsals. There was no doubt about it, it was going to be exhausting and hard work, and some of the girls also needed time out to sit their GCSE exams. On our first day of rehearsals, the most important thing of all was to get to know each other. After putting the girls into line, I showed them the correct way to place their arms around each other's waist – oh yes, there is a special way of doing this, even though it was one of the smallest of details required for a Tiller Girls' routine. This was necessary for perfection.

The opening routine of any show is probably the most important, and usually the one number an audience will remember. When the assembly are shown to their seats, some of them may have been sitting there for, say, a good ten minutes or more waiting to be entertained and wondering what will greet them when the curtain goes up. For me as a professional dancer, I felt we were warming the audience up for more spectacular things to come, and judging by our reception on most occasions, we set the goals high.

Back to rehearsals. As the new line of Tillers heard the music for their opening routine, they had a look of disbelief on their faces. As they started to learn their routine, they couldn't believe the tempo of the music. They were horrified and looked at me as if I was playing a trick on them. This was something they were going to have to master. A Tiller Girls' routine was always very slick, fast and persuasive. It was skilfully devised and carried out with perfect precision, being accurate in every detail, with strict observing rules.

Over the next three days their tempo began to improve and fall into place, but not without the usual pulled and stiff muscles and blisters on their feet. By day five they had learnt five routines, with not much time to clean things up, and during short coffee and tea breaks, they also had costume fittings. Part of day five was also taken up with the principals and Mr Danny La Rue. The girls were introduced into a couple of their routines. Along with the girls, they had to learn their moves; these were called production numbers which were performed with the company.

On day six we had our dress rehearsal. This was a time when you performed in full costume with the band, and when you found out what you could and couldn't do. Things always felt unusually different once you had your costume, new shoes and headdress on. During rehearsals you always wore your comfy clothes and shoes. At this point you would discover whether you needed extra hairgrips or tighter elastic on your headdress if it had fallen off or was swinging round your neck. You would search out if you had enough time to do your quick change, and discover if extra music was needed to get across the stage to exit.

I personally can remember going to pieces and being in fear that I wouldn't make a quick change. In fright, I pulled my headdress off my head and a huge amount of hair with it. By the end of the season I ended up with a bald patch on my head. If one girl could make a quick change, they could all do it, even if she was very experienced.

I was hoping this wouldn't happen, but I wasn't surprised; yes, we had a problem with the music. It wasn't entirely the girls' fault; they were struggling with the tempo, but the band seemed to be striving to keep up with the drummer. After a short while, this solution was solved. I remember this happening on the odd occasion when we did our band call for a Sunday Night at the Palladium TV Show. Jack Parnell, our musical director, would play our music too fast. We thought it was so they could save a few seconds of time as the show went out live.

With our dress rehearsal over and most problems solved, it was now make or break time. There was no more time left and the big night had arrived. As I helped the girls to get into their opening costumes for their Big Night, I wished them good luck, or as we say in the business "break a leg", hardly an inspiring thing to say to a Tiller Girl!! I walked down the corridor past the portacabins of the principals' dressing rooms. I knocked on each door and thanked them for their hard work and wished them a big success. As I wandered out into the auditorium to take my seat, I thought "if there's one thing I regret, it's that mum and dad didn't live long enough to see me achieve their dream". I'd achieved mine. It would have been so wonderful to have them sitting by me on this momentous night.

It was forty-three years ago that mum just wanted her daughter to be a Tiller Girl. On this most special, important, significant night of my life, I was sitting in the audience with my friend Kath by my side. She was one of my close Tiller Girl friends who gave me much support. While waiting for the show to begin, Kath and I realised how the girls would be feeling, and even though we weren't on stage, I was experiencing the nerves and butterflies in my stomach. As the music started and the overture began to introduce the Tiller Girls, the Palladium music blared out loudly into the auditorium. Both Kath and I experienced opening night nervousness. As the girls came on stage performing their high kicks, I felt a bundle of fibres in the base of my stomach. I tried to remain calm, but the anxiety and tension was making me feel apprehensive. I didn't want to start the applause, I wanted the girls to be worthy of their deserving admiration. Then I heard what I was waiting for, the tremendous applause of approval from the audience, and they sounded as if they had an appetite for more.

During the applause my heart swelled with pride and love: pride that I had achieved my lifelong ambition; it gave me happiness and ultimate joy. I remember thinking, is this really happening, is it a dream, make believe or fairytale? The love I felt was for this wonderful line of dancers that I had auditioned, trained and choreographed and who I hoped our mentor, John Tiller, would have approved of. I couldn't relax. There were times when the girls were performing that I felt all of a flutter, and the rush of colour caused me to become red faced. My body felt on fire; I was certainly having a hot flush.

When we came to the finale, which was very colourful, bright with sequins and feathers, I felt a sigh of relief. The audience showed their appreciation by their tremendous applause. Then when Mr Danny La Rue had finally taken his bow and the whole company came forward to join him, the rush of enthusiasm and standing ovation, cheers and applause greeted the whole company.

As the audience left their seats, through the crowds Kath and I made our way back stage. I overheard the conversations coming from the audience as they made their way to the exit. I heard how much they had enjoyed the show and how wonderful it was to see the Tiller Girls back performing. It was comforting to me to hear these remarks.

I was still on tender hooks and anxious to hear the feedback from our producer, Mr Duggie Chapman, and the star of the show, Mr Danny La Rue, but at this point, the stars of the show for me were the Tiller Girls. As we arrived back stage in the hospitality area champagne was freely flowing. Out of the corner of my eye I could see Mr Danny La Rue and Mr Chapman. As they came towards me, I flashed a warm smile. I was on edge, and be it good or bad, I was prepared for criticism. I felt as if I was waiting to be assessed and being marked on an examination, but it wasn't like that at all. They both greeted me with warm and pleasing smiles, and the charm from Mr Danny La Rue who was still in his distinguished character and full stage make-up, flung his arms around me and kissed me on the cheek. I felt his long fluttery eyelashes brush over my face. His remark was "well done Fay" and he seemed elated and overjoyed. Mr Chapman was equally delighted, and congratulated me on everyone's remarkable performance. It was nice there had been no major hold-up or delays, and he handed me an envelope with a cheque inside!

As the season came to an end, on the last night Mr Danny La Rue gave me a beautiful evening bag and card to say a big thank you. Danny was a very generous person. As well as the memories, these are things I cherish dearly.

Not long as the show had finished, I received a phone call from Mr Chapman. We were in conversation to bring the show back to Blackpool the following year (2001) for a second summer season, but this time we were to cut the number of performances in the week and take the show on tour at the week-ends. This meant that on occasions the routines had to be changed, depending on the size of the stage, and of course this involved a lot of travelling. I was "over the moon" to be asked back for a second year. I thought it was very brave of Mr Chapman to take the show on the road, being as we were still in a recession. To me this seemed a brilliant idea. If for any reason the public couldn't get to a show, take the show to the people! How wonderful.

Although the show had Danny La Rue topping the bill and was similar to the previous year of 2000, there were a few changes. Instead of 12 Tiller Girls, we had 10 Tillers. The routines all had to be altered and this made formations more difficult having an odd number to work with. There were two new production numbers for Mr La Rue: a "clown" routine and "Diamonds are a Girl's Best Friend", and the girls did a Bob Fosse type routine. There was still plenty to do with, once again, a short rehearsal time.

I took time out from my beauty business. I closed my salon for one week to audition for one or two replacements, re-choreograph the routines and new production numbers, and another successful show went out on the road.

With the recession still biting hard, work for dancers was becoming sparse, especially for Tiller Girls. It became too expensive to employ twelve girls and kit them out in shoes, costumes and feathers. The only work now available was on cruise ships or, if you were a good individual dancer, in a musical. Height now didn't seem to matter; it was all about your dancing and singing ability.

I feel I've made a part of the Tiller Girls' history, having been a longstanding Tiller Girl myself, and choreographed for the Tiller Girls' unique style of dance, and having put the production numbers together without bringing in an outside choreographer. I think my parents and family would have been proud, and I would hope John Tiller would have been, too.

Scene Sixteen

Buckingham Palace Garden Party

In July 2004 it was a great honour to be invited to the Garden Party at Buckingham Palace for the NOT FORGOTTEN ASSOCIATION.

I think this invitation was to show appreciation for all our charity work, which is still ongoing. We all got ourselves glammed up in our outdoor clothes, not our usual feathers and sequins! It was a very memorable and exciting day. What a wonderful experience it was driving my car through Buckingham Palace gates, parking at the side of the Palace, walking through the Palace and out into the back garden. The atmosphere was truly amazing. We walked down to the bottom of the garden by the lake, and all the Tillers posed for photographs. While we enjoyed our sandwiches, strawberries and cream tea, we watched the guards and band march up and down the lawn. There were lots of celebrities present, and we were in the company of our Princess Royal who mingled among the crowds.

One of the nice things, too, was we could take a guest, and I took my sister-in-law, Beverly. On leaving the Palace she made me laugh. As we drove towards the Palace gates to exit, Beverly said slow down while I phone Jeremy (my brother). She said we are just leaving the Palace as we drove through the gates. It had been an exciting and most beautiful day to remember, and so nice to have a member of my family to share this special occasion with.

*Mingling with the staff in the back garden of Buckingham Palace.
I'm looking for the girls.*

*Down by the lake with other guests.
I'm on the end on the right, my usual working position.*

Scene Seventeen

My Thousand Sisters

Life as a John Tiller Girl wasn't always glamorous and well paid. When you had made it to the Palladium Line-up you were very lucky and were offered further contracts, say, for Saturday Startime Television and the Billy Cotton Band Shows. Only then did we feel we were financially better off.

Television work paid a set fee both for rehearsals and transmission. It all came with a price: there were no days off! We sometimes travelled over night by coach or train from wherever we were working, arriving in London in the early hours of the morning at the Palladium or studio, having had no sleep and turning up ready for our day's rehearsal and transmission. It wouldn't be allowed or expected of you today. How we looked became a problem because television could add a stone to your body weight. Many girls struggled with this, and in fear of being taken from the TV troupe would spend their extra pennies on attending slimming clinics to keep their weight down; some even referred to taking slimming pills.

Some dancers would not obey the strict rules of discipline. They wouldn't be offered a second contract. Our rehearsal uniform always included our famous black Tiller bow. Some new recruits would not be tamed; they had no wish to look alike which conflicted with the Tiller's concept. They would not see the sense behind the rule, and would refuse to put themselves out! Once, a dedicated Tiller realised she had forgotten her Tiller's precious black bow. Not wanting to face the discipline, without hesitation, although it might cost her half her salary, she took a return trip by taxi to her digs to get it.

Trousers were considered smart in the fifties and sixties and were becoming fashionable in everyday life, but for some reason Tillers were banned from wearing them. As usual, a newcomer would not learn about the rule until she had broken it, then she would hear from Miss Barbara "never trousers, my dear". There we were in the early sixties with our mini skirts halfway up our bums and in the street hotpants were being worn (I had a hotpants suit) yet the Tillers headquarters thought trousers were indecent.

Some rules were compulsory: for example, hair must be short and well groomed and off the collar, and we could not change the colour. In order to enforce the rule, there was a specific paragraph typed down the side of our contracts. Lacquer became our best friend as it seemed to solve some problems. Miss Barbara hated to see our hair bouncing up and down. Sometimes, worried of being told to get it cut, we sprayed so heavily our hair became as stiff as a board and would stick to our headdress. This helped to keep the headdress on, but sometimes we couldn't get the damn thing off.

At times life was like being in the Army. We had to be prepared to go wherever we were sent at a moment's notice if we were asked to replace a Tiller in another troupe until they found a suitable replacement.

Towards the end of a season, a longstanding Tiller was usually offered a further contract. It was normally a routine for the office to keep a good troupe together which is what happened with the sixties girls. I got the feeling that if you turned a contract down, the office got suspicious of you and wondered what you were up to. When performing for a season, we would wait for one another and follow each other down the stairs on to the stage. During rehearsals our feet would be killing us, our shoes too tight from swollen feet and blisters, so if ever there was a lull and we were standing around in costume, we would wait for one Tiller to make a move and sit down, then we would follow suit. We clung to each other like peas in a pod – like sisters do!

In Blackpool and in my early twenties, I started to show an interest in boys. For the first time in my life, someone was showing a desire, fondness and liking for me. I was longing to be cherished and shown love and affection, but at the end of the season I was offered a contract to captain a troupe of Tillers going out to South Africa. I couldn't have been sent further away – had someone spilt the beans, I guess so.

I turned the contract down and asked if I could do north of the border. "No" was the reply "you know why you can't go north", no questions asked. Most dancers would have jumped at the offer. I realised a few days later what a wonderful opportunity it was to see the world and be paid for it, visiting Johannesburg, Durban, Pretoria, Port Elizabeth, Cape Town and Bulawayo. The contract was short, only three months, so I changed my mind. I was told yes I could go but the captaincy had been offered to someone else. I felt I had been punished for having a boyfriend. Although in my mid-twenties, if a grown up woman was in a serious relationship it seemed to be deliberately wrecked by the simple method of never letting couples work together, although one or two were lucky and did escape the rule. We never did find out what the ruling was on boyfriends as no-one would dare ask. It was very noticeable that there wasn't any or many married girls in a troupe. We soon learnt to keep things quiet.

Before we left for South Africa we were called to the officer where we had a race to the skip to find shoes and costumes (which were well worn). We tried to look for a costume that had our name in it which had been crossed out several times and had been worn by a Tiller Girl from previous troupes. Our shoes and costumes had been worn by hundreds of girls.

On arriving in Johannesburg, it was thought the high altitude would defeat us. Oxygen cylinders were situated on side stage in case we needed them. The high altitude was about 6,000 feet above sea level. If we found ourselves breathless, we knew the cylinders were there. Sometimes breathing normal was out of the question at the end of our routines. As we made for the exit and reached the wings gasping for breath, our first move was to clear the wings and unzip each other's costumes.

The hotel we stayed in was very basic but clean. We never wandered far; like sisters, always together. In the day we lazed around the pool and at night we would be taken to the theatre by 'limo'; all twelve of us piled in like sardines in a tin. In the early sixties there was still conflict with the black and white South Africans, with special buses and entrances to shops for each. In Cape Town we even did separate shows for all black audiences and all whites. In between shows we played board games, cards and chequers with each other and other members of the cast, being Keith Harris and Mike and Bernie Winters.

In Johannesburg we experienced many earth tremors. Being on the top floor of the hotel was frightening. The pictures on the walls were swinging from side to side and cups were sliding across the table. You could feel the building swaying, and it was a relief when it was over.

When our tour took us to the coastline of Port Elizabeth and Durban, we had the bonus of a beautiful sandy beach which was a short walk from our hotel. Here we would all meet and wander down to the beach. The experienced swimmers of the troupe would enjoy a daily swim, but one day an almost tragic accident happened. As the girls were enjoying their swim, Sue, one of them, seemed to be drifting further out and the non-swimmers, myself being one of them, were getting very agitated. We watched nervously as she appeared to disappear. In fright and panic we ran to the water's edge shouting her name, "Sue, Sue, come back". Then with sudden overwhelming fear we ran to two guys, one joined us shouting for help while the other alerted the Beach Patrol. By now we had lost Sue and didn't have sight of her. We were now desperate as we realised she had reached the shark nets and wires, and in despair, we were hoping she hadn't been taken over on to the other side. The Beach Patrol was on the way, and at the water's edge there was a line of Tiller Girls in tears.

As the patrol reached the wire netting which Sue was tangled in, they lifted her onboard. We were all desperately hoping she was still with us. When they brought her in and lifted her from the boat covered in blood from the wires which had ripped at her arms and legs as she struggled to hold on, there was big relief and gladness when we heard her talk. She wasn't in tears or hysterical, she seemed quite calm but exhausted and in shock. She'd used every bit of her strength and energy to survive. Later when she was asked why she went out so far, she said the current of the sea was dragging her out; the more she tried to get back the sea was pulling her out, and Sue was a good swimmer. I don't think we went in the sea again. She had a very lucky escape.

In the fifties and sixties there was plenty of work for the Tiller Girls and other dancers. The Tillers had their unique style of dancing with their highly distinctive routines, and having been ballet, tap, character, acrobatic and modern musically trained at local dancing schools where they lived, but we lacked the new American style that was now taking place. The problem was, how could we acquire this skill? The only answer was to attend modern dance classes. We had many, many opportunities to learn new choreography with a variety of styles. As explained earlier in my story, when we were booked for the big shows, an outside choreographer was employed to arrange the production numbers. This made it possible to learn different styles of dance and bring out any hidden talents within each individual Tiller. At times this was frightening, especially for me. My shyness held me back. I never would push myself forward to the front line in case anyone thought I was showing off, and I lacked the courage needed. These outside choreographers were given a line of Tiller Girls to work with, but they were not their choice of girls. Miss Barbara would audition her dancers for the work they were required to do. The choreographers who were brought in didn't have that choice, and were given dancers (Tillers) they hadn't auditioned who they hoped could do their style of dance. Bearing in mind they would have their name on the bill as having choreographed the show, it was a big responsibility for them.

I suppose it was just as hard for us to have to adapt ourselves accordingly. Some choreographers it was a pleasure to work with: Malcolm Goddard, Lionel Blair and Ken Martyn we adored. They had a kind of charming way of talking to us and made rehearsal times enjoyable and a learning curve with opportunities to learn different techniques. Malcolm Goddard was a darling; his style was very glamorous and suited most dancers, with a sexy walk, swinging arms which showed off our diamante bracelets. Ken Martyn was funny and often made us laugh. He would give us steps to do on the right hand stage and tell us to reverse if on the left.

At the other end of the scale were Fred Peters and George Carden. I believe Fred Peters used to assist Pam Devies who was always very polite towards us. Her dancers performed alternate Sundays during the late sixties at Sunday Night at The Palladium. Miss Devies always set the finale of the show as she was the resident choreographer. In the early years the Palladium TV shows were dominated by George Carden who could be bitter and sarcastic at times. I first met up with him in 1957 when I did my first Sunday Night Palladium TV Series. He seemed to have very little patience, and I once heard Fred Peters' Dancers saying he used to throw things at them. I wasn't sure if they mentioned a chair. This made me feel on edge when working with them.

Joan Davies was my very first outside choreographer while working as a Tiller Girl in the Big Show at the Opera House Blackpool. Miss Davies could either love you or hate you. Some of the girls knew she had a soft spot for blondes. I wasn't blonde at the time. She was a stocky "butch" lady, not very tall with short legs, but she could travel across that big Opera House stage with a few strides. I undoubtedly made a lasting impression on her. Being very young and painfully shy, I walked to the back of the stage to hide behind the others. Miss Davies smiled and said "come forward my dear, yes you, come down to the front". From then on I could do no wrong. I must have been on good terms with her because she gave me a little solo spot at the beginning of the production number. If she didn't like you, she would make sure you would be dancing behind a pillar or piece of scenery. There was one thing she did teach us: while waiting in the wings on side stage to make our entrance, Miss Davies, sitting in the stalls, would shout "Girls, get out of sight, if you can see the audience they can see you". That has always stuck in my mind (all through my show business career) and became a valuable piece of information.

Joan Davies asked one of our girls where she came from. Her reply was "The Grandison College". We all let out a huge unarticulated sound of laughter. We were so amused; this particular girl spoke quite posh which made it more amusing. What Miss Davies actually meant was where had she come from on stage.

The War Years

When I accepted my first contract with the Tiller Girls, I was always very quiet. I would listen a lot, take it all in and say nothing. I was once in conversation with one of the older girls who was telling us stories and what it was like for the Tillers during the war. Most of the work on offer involved touring so problems arose with the basics of life.

Ration books were issued, and as they trailed around looking for food, because they were dancers and muttered to each other, they tried to charm the shopkeepers into giving them extra food, and often waltzed out of the shop with something special to eat. Anxious mothers sent whatever food and clothing they could lay their hands on. It wasn't unusual to receive a parcel with cakes and clothes together. It took me back to when I received my weekly parcel from my dancing teachers with food in it when I was in London and stayed at the Theatre Girls Club. Fortunately, there were many invitations to parties during the war so they were able to ward off starvation. The only query they raised before accepting was "will there be food?"

This became a joke among the Tillers and still is today. They went to the parties simply because of the food which had been flown in. They weren't interested in smoking, they weren't allowed to anyway, or talking to Americans. They would take their carrier bags and fill them, then sit waiting wondering when they could go home only five minutes after they had arrived. Food seemed to have always played a big part in a Tiller Girl's life. At any event, if ever you were looking for one of the Tiller Girls, you'd ask where the food was and you'd always find her there. On arrival at a venue we would always discuss when would it be the best time to eat. So since the war things haven't changed much in the food department.

During the war all round the country theatre shows carried on through the air raids. No-one ever left the theatre, even when the bombs dropped, and it was quite usual to stay in the theatre till two or three in the morning. London was undoubtedly the worst hit of all the places the Tiller Girls worked. When booked for Hackney Empire, Shepherds Bush and Finsbury Park Empire during the heavy phase, the raids continued on till morning, and the girls had to sleep in the theatre most nights.

First the sirens would give them the warning, an announcement would follow: "Ladies and gentlemen, if you wish to leave the theatre please do". No-one ever did, they were probably safer in the theatre than taking a risk and leaving. The show continued as explosions lit up the sky and fire engines raced up the streets as buildings collapsed. If the "all clear" had not been given by the time they had done the finale, artistes would continue with their improvisational skills. When exhausted, the audience would often take over. When the "all clear" was given and the artistes and audience were able to leave, a few of the Tiller Girls found they had lost their entire families while working away from home, yet I'd heard not one Tiller was killed while on contract.

Within months of war being declared, clothes became more practical and boiler suits were popular. Clothes were in such short supply and life was slowed down by the time spent queuing for necessities with ration books and clothes coupons. When I was a little girl, mum made most of our clothes. She would have us all dressed the same, even the boys: rompers with a bib and braces, and a short box type top that tied at the front. The oldest of us all would get new and then they were handed down. When I was about twelve years old I had a pale blue coat which after two years, covered in marks, faded with wear, mum decided to revive. She dyed it donkey brown (along with a few other things) and sewed on a new set of buttons. I had a new coat. Donkey brown became very popular. It became a common thing to find forty or fifty women queuing for clothes and shoes.

I shopped with ration books and queued with coupons. When I was eight years old clothes came off ration. It was make do and mend. Our parents and grandparents would darn our socks and sew patches over the holes of the knees of my bothers' trousers. The men's trousers were quite big and baggy, and with my granddad's trousers my gran made skirts. Gran and mum could make anything, and sewing became part of our family life which we all learnt to dabble in. At least we knew no-one else would be wearing the same.

In the late fifties and for many years I performed in a Tiller troupe in a special cabaret every October for the El-Alimain Reunion at the Festival Hall in London with Field Marshall General Montgomery, known as Monty. Every year Dame Vera Lynn was present. It was such an eventful, memorable evening and a great honour to be asked.

Performing annually in this show always brought back the memories of the war years. Being around at that time made you appreciate and value life and realise how lucky you were to live to tell the tale.

Scene Eighteen

A Love For My Work

I enjoyed working as a Beauty Therapist for a further eight years. I had small gaps when I did my charity work and performed with my beloved "sisters" (The 60s Tiller Girls) which I was able to do because I worked for myself.

In 2009 I decided to retire. I was now sixty eight years old. When retirement was mentioned to my clients, the question arose "can I do a list of mobile?" I was now put in a difficult position. Not only was I reluctant to let go of my work, my customers didn't want me to give up either. I spent a few weeks gathering interest from my clientele, and was flabbergasted by the response. I had over forty ladies showing a huge interest. I'd now decided there could be a market for my customers' needs and for me as a part-time mobile Beauty Therapist. It meant I could continue doing what I enjoyed at a time that suited both my clients and me. So I went "mobile" and started working a few hours a week.

Over the years, on a number of occasions, I've bumped into several gym members from the health club. They would always approach me with "we would love you to come back and do a class for us". I was still keen on fitness, which I've never given up on. I've always been self-motivated and kept up my exercises. I said I would phone Mr Birchall, the health club owner, and see what he says. I thought I would love to do it and the gamble would only be a yes or no. His reply was that he would be delighted. It was nice to give something back to a place which had made me very happy, and I decided to give my services voluntarily and bring happiness to the members.

The social side of doing my mobile and taking my fitness class, callanetics and pilates was fantastic; it warmed me when clients complimented me on my professionalism. Nothing usually goes wrong, but if it does, the key to success is practice or, in some cases, laugh and have fun. I put a lot of love in what I do which makes it rewarding.

Vision Impairment

In April 2010 my sight was beginning to give me concern. I was having double vision in my left eye, and as I could see a person, their face and features would disappear. It was making me feel less confident, and I would prevent myself from doing things because I couldn't see properly; even with my reading glasses on I was having difficulty.

I made an appointment with my optician for an eye test. I thought I may need new lenses and spectacles. He immediately said I needed to see an eye specialist as I had a problem with the cornea. He faxed a letter straightaway to the hospital, and an appointment was made for the following morning.

The specialist asked if I had had a knock or bang on the eye, which I hadn't. The only bang I could recall was when I was still at school when my teacher threw a bunch of keys at me. I had lots of tests and scans taken on both eyes, one being a retinal angiography where a dye was injected into my bloodstream via a vein in my arm and photographs taken of the vessels at the back of my eyes. I was warned that the fluorescein dye would turn my skin a yellow brown colour. When I left the hospital I looked as if I'd just returned from the Bahamas.

The results of the test confirmed that I needed a small operation to cut the vitreous jelly away. This clear transparent jelly is cut from the inside of the eye. The operation is called a vitrectomy. The vitreous humour or jelly is situated behind the iris, the coloured part of the eye, and in front of the retina at the back of the eye. It has no real function other than providing packaging inside the eye. This jelly had attached itself to the back of my eye and was pulling on the retina. I had a general anaesthetic and stayed overnight in hospital.

I must say that when I was taken down to the theatre I felt very tearful and frightened that I may lose my sight. I took deep breaths and appeared to be brave, but I was very nervous and hoped I'd made the right decision. This all sounds a lot more complicated than it actually was. It was virtually painless, apparent from being a bit sore and bloodshot, and I began to wonder why I had got myself all worked up.

On my next appointment with my surgeon I was sent for further tests. The whole procedure was done in my other eye, but this time I felt a little more comfortable about it. I was warned that cataracts would appear sooner rather than later. Soon after, my sight deteriorated again; driving became impossible, faces were disappearing, colours were faded, and I found myself wearing dark glasses constantly. I went back to the surgeon to get both my cataracts removed. I thought this would be the end of my hospital visits as my vision had improved and my specialist said my sight was now about as good as it would get. I felt quite happy with my vision for a few weeks, and it was nice to see things in a different light. Then, six months later, things began to fade, white was grey,

I was losing brightness, colour and strength, and things seemed to be vanishing slowly before my eyes. I made a trip back to the opticians and then to the hospital; I was a bit apprehensive to know what had gone wrong. It appeared to be the cataract lenses that had steamed up at the back of my eyes so it was like I was looking through a steamed-up window. I was calmly told that this only happens to about 2% of people, but that it could be all sorted with laser treatment. I had both eyes lasered with excellent results and instant vision. As soon as I'd had the treatment I wiped my eyes, and as I opened them I said "WOW" and thanked God for answering my prayers.

I couldn't believe the brightness, the colours, the definition: black was black! When I arrived home I saw every crumb on the kitchen floor. I looked at myself in the mirror and I was horrified. I looked twenty years older: every wrinkle was twice the size. I'd been looking at myself as if I'd been airbrushed. I'm pleased to say I've been very lucky as I now only require glasses for reading which is wonderful. I'm now getting used to seeing my wrinkles and not looking like an airbrushed celebrity any more. I'm more than grateful to have my sight back and see all things in a different light.

There have been stepping stones for me on every journey through my life. It could be good feedback from my boss or a customer, or perhaps I've solved a crisis at work before it ever started. A mantra such as "well done, keep up the good work" is so much more effective in building confidence than finding the things that went wrong, the mistakes and the imperfections on every journey. I give myself small rewards: a walk on the beach, a day out with friends, buy something new or take a yoga class to relax and make me feel good.